M000072960

PRAISE FOR NINA SIMONS AND
NATURE, CULTURE AND THE SACRED

The world seems to be divided into two kinds of people—those who divide everything into two, and those who don't. Reading *Nature, Culture and the Sacred* is a step toward melting this false division into "feminine" and "masculine," and allowing each of us to become fully human again and at last.

> — **Gloria Steinem**, co-founder of *Ms. Magazine*

In *Nature, Culture and the Sacred* Nina Simons has woven a compelling and honest tapestry of hard-earned personal and collective wisdom, honoring the earth and igniting the revolutionary ways of women. It's a book as much about the inside as it is about the outside, exploring where and how they can meet for a sustainable future.

> — **Eve Ensler**, founder of V-Day and author of *The Vagina Monologues*

Nature, Culture and the Sacred: A Woman Listens for Leadership is the perfect book for this historical moment. Nina Simons not only knows the rare gifts of leadership women can offer, she also reveals how challenge and adversity bring these gifts forth more brilliantly and powerfully.

> — **Joanna Macy**, author of *World As Lover, World As Self*

With characteristic grace and great insight, Nina Simons shows us another path for leadership, one that grows from intuition, emotional intelligence and, above all, connection in every form, including human relationship. This book is a treasure chest of both knowledge and know-how, giving us what we all need, women and men alike: a larger vision with which together we can save the Earth and ourselves from the devastation that comes from the sadly more narrow and impoverished ways of seeing we mistake for reality. This book is the real thing.

— **Susan Griffin**, author of *Woman and Nature* and *The Roaring Inside Her*

Nina Simons listened to the call of her soul and stepped into her role of waking women up to the need to embrace their leadership abilities. *Nature, Culture, and the Sacred* shares a wealth of insights to assist us in replacing the old worn-out patriarchal and hierarchical paradigm. Simons brilliantly discusses the issues involved, shares moving stories of women around the world joining together to create change, as well as weaving in teachings from Indigenous cultures of how to reconnect people, nature, and the land. This is an amazing book that will inspire our current population of women and generations to come. It is an important book to help us ride the waves of change.

— **Sandra Ingerman**, author of *Soul Retrieval* and *Walking in Light: The Everyday Empowerment of Shamanic Life*

This is the time when the power of women returns to us, as we reaffirm our relationships to each other and to our Mother Earth. Together we will doula the next economy into being, re-birthing ourselves and this world. Nina's writing explores the path forward on this journey that we will make together.

— **Winona LaDuke**, Executive Director, Honor the Earth

I especially appreciate the foregrounding of Indigenous wisdom and Indigenous elders and teachers in Nina's work at Bioneers and Cultivating Women's Leadership. *Nature, Culture and the Sacred* underscores the urgent necessity of shifting our awareness away from the stories that have kept us separate, alienated and divided throughout the centuries of modernity. I can't wait to recommend this book for Leadership courses at the university and to everyone in my circles! The poetic riffs in some of the chapters induce a kind of reverie that kindles the fire in my heart and suffuses me with longing for a future worth waiting for. May it be. Bathala Nawa.

> — **Leny Mendoza Strobel**, author and associate professor of American Multicultural Studies, Sonoma State University

To be a whole human being is to live our connection, our unity with all life, people and the Earth. Nina Simons' messages in Nature, Culture and the Sacred remind us how to end needless suffering and embrace our wholeness.

> — **Dr. Anita Sanchez**, international bestselling author, *The Four Sacred Gifts: Indigenous Wisdom for Modern Times*

Nature, Culture and the Sacred invites all of us into a new way of living, loving and leading in the world; one that embraces the quest towards wholeness, honors the commitment to full integrity and celebrates the courage of true alignment. Nina has given us a gorgeous roadmap, paving the way towards greater self-love, appreciation and acceptance, all of which are sorely needed to lead in these times. Thank you, dear Nina, for this marvelous work.

> — **Rha Goddess**, Founder of Move The Crowd and author of *The Calling*

Nature, culture and the Sacred

A WOMAN LISTENS
FOR LEADERSHIP

For my beloved friend
Mary, with endless
love, admiration
and in sisterhood

Nina

Properly footnoted quotations of up to 500 sequential words may be used without permission, granted the total number of words quoted does not exceed 2,000.
For longer quotations, or for a greater number of total words, please contact Green Fire Press:
PO Box 377 Housatonic MA 01236
www.greenfirepress.com
info@greenfirepress.org

Cover art: *Samantabhadra on Bike* by Mayumi Oda
Interior and cover art by CBB Designs
Page design by CBB Designs and Anna Myers Sabatini

Library of Congress Control Number: 2018961890
ISBN: 978-1-7328414-0-6

Simons, Nina.
Nature, culture and the sacred : a woman listens for leadership / Nina Simons ; edited by Anneke Campbell.
Housatonic, MA : Green Fire Press, [2019], ©2019.
239 pages ; 23 cm
978-1-7328414-0-6
1. Simons, Nina. 2. Leadership in women. 3. Women social reformers.
4.Women environmentalists. 5. Women in development.
6. Social action.
I. Campbell, Anneke.
HQ1123 .S56 2019
303.48/4082 (23 ed.)

Nature, Culture and the Sacred

A WOMAN LISTENS FOR LEADERSHIP

Nina Simons

edited by Anneke Campbell

Green
Fire
Press

TABLE OF CONTENTS

Nature, Culture and the Sacred

A WOMAN LISTENS FOR LEADERSHIP

INTRODUCTION

When I turned 40, I began receiving public acknowledgement for my leadership in Bioneers, featuring and making visible the innovative leaders, stories and visions related to sustainability. At the time, I had a very ambivalent response to being named a leader. I knew that I should feel honored, but instead found that I felt anxious and conflicted.

As I shared my experience with friends and colleagues, most of them women, I discovered they too felt similarly conflicted about leadership as an aspiration or public persona. At the same time, I knew leadership from all quarters was hugely needed to address the social and ecological crises we were headed toward, so this incongruity plagued me. From that point forward I began a twenty-year exploration into the nature of leadership and its reinvention, an inquiry that has shaped my life ever since.

I began by unpacking my own internal definition of leadership. I wondered whether unconscious stories, roles, cultural biases or societal definitions might be contributing to the discomfort I was feeling.

In my mind, my previously unexamined assumption was that leaders tended to be characterized as solitary, accomplished and self-assured individuals who held final power and ultimate authority. They often worked to the point of sickness or exhaustion, and were inclined toward lifestyles of self-sacrifice. I also assumed that any leader existed within a hierarchical or dominator framework.

I started seeing that my culturally inherited definition of leadership was predicated upon a social assumption of competition, hierarchy and scarcity. As I scanned the leadership landscape, I saw how much of what I deeply aspired to for my own evolution didn't match up with what was conventionally being modeled. I noticed that appearances, stature, scale and outer achievement were much more highly honored in leaders than inner awareness, mindfulness, integrity or deep listening. I saw how certitude was a prevalent attitude among conventional leaders, with little room for questioning.

I observed how analytical and procedural thinking was typically more highly praised than creative, relational and innovative thinking. I recalled that Carl Jung ascribed the archetypal feminine to our interiority, and the masculine to our exteriority. I began to see that the imbalance that was true within me — of valuing my more "masculine" traits and undervaluing those I ascribed to the archetypal "feminine" within me — was also present within other people, men and women, as well as in our institutions and social structures. I also saw how valuable it could be to awaken people — especially women — to that internal bias, to be better able to shed or transform it in us all.

Indigenous peoples of the Amazon believe that the bird of humanity has flown on only one wing for far too long, notes Lynne Twist, who runs the Soul of Money Institute and co-founded the Pachamama Alliance. These times, they say, require that the feminine fully join the masculine so that the bird of humanity can gain full wing, flying to soar with its whole capacity.

But when I looked at what the concepts "masculine" and "feminine" meant to me, I could see that during my early professional career, I had presented first from my masculine side, making sure to appear capable, qualified, stable, focused and self-assured. I was quick, rational and decisive. I prided myself on how much I could accomplish each day. When I didn't know the answer to a question or how to do something, I employed bravado, making up a response or solution, while hoping it would turn out well. I rarely admitted to being uncertain or needing more information or time to consider.

Inwardly, of course, I was sometimes unsure, nervous or emotionally variable. Within myself, I discounted many of the other qualities that served me as a leader: my ability to listen deeply, empathize and connect, my skill at collaboration, my capacity to see, encourage and inspire the leadership of others, and my contextual awareness of potential impacts to the whole systems involved.

I vowed that going forward I would live more explicitly integrating my feminine side, since we all contain a full spectrum of aspects within ourselves, regardless of our gender. As a leader, I wanted my toolkit to encompass all of my human capacities, and to be able to draw from anywhere on that spectrum at any given time, marrying apparent contradictions: for instance, being focused and decisive while considering full contextual and relational implications. I came to see that having access to a full array of my human capacities allowed me to show up in the world in a more authentic and effective way. It permitted me to bring more aspects of myself into my daily life and interactions.

That full-spectrum approach also gave me a greater capacity for renewing myself after periods of intense productivity. I discovered that the feminine within me needs periods of rest and reflection, spacious time to re-inhabit my body, heart and spirit, which revitalizes me. I discovered that integrating even brief times for rest into my daily routine led me to be able to feel better resourced and nourished, throughout my days.

In considering full-spectrum leadership, I noted the extent to which our U.S. culture tends to avoid what's difficult, vulnerable or painful. We chronically tend to deny, avoid or medicate the kinds of inner turmoil that can lead to real personal growth. Shadow is defined psychologically as unconscious aspects of our personality, which the ego does not acknowledge.

Without bringing those aspects into awareness, they exert undue and often unconscious influence upon our actions. Our collective aversion to experiencing grief and depression also fits into this overall bias. I saw that without facing, valuing and integrating our personal and collective shadows we might be doomed to recycling our wounds and to a perpetual personal and emotional immaturity.

I yearned to reinvent and reclaim a new form of leadership that we might all aspire to. Seeking models, I looked to people from the Bioneers networks from different disciplines, backgrounds and walks of life, and at different stages in their leadership or life journeys. These exemplary leaders, many of whom you will meet in the essays that follow, were creative and collaborative, curious and courageous, humble and passionate, and had diverse, yet authentic responses to the challenges their work posed. They merged the rational with the intuitive, at once. They wove the relational, the strategic and the collaborative — and were able to balance deep listening, openness and humility with asserting their own understanding, or what they knew to be true.

Some may not have even considered themselves leaders. Regardless of what they were called, what I found was that those who most inspired me were the ones who didn't necessarily have a title, graduate degree, or external markers of authority.

What they had was a passionate commitment to some aspect of the living world, and that dedication or love was so profound that it caused them to act with a dignified authority. It was like they'd received an assignment from their intuition, heart or spirit. They might not have called it that, but it was as if their inner voice said, "I have to do something to protect or defend or reinvent what I love."

Reflecting on these new models of leadership led me to co-edit (with Anneke Campbell) the book *Moonrise: The Power of Women Leading from the Heart*, an anthology of more than 30 essays from a collection of diverse women (and some men) trailblazers that has been widely read and employed in university and graduate courses about leadership, women and diversity.

I was also inspired to co-create the Cultivating Women's Leadership (CWL) intensives in 2006 with Toby Herzlich and Akaya Windwood, two longtime facilitators and transformative process designers with deep life experience both with women and leadership trainings. These six-day residential intensives, housed within Bioneers, were designed to: clarify each woman's sense of purpose; experience beloved community among a very diverse group; explore the shadow side of women's leadership; develop intentional practices for ongoing self-cultivation; and offer women an embodied experience of how powerfully and quickly women can accelerate one another's learning and leadership capacities.

Co-facilitating the Cultivating Women's Leadership intensives (most recently in partnership with co-founder Toby Herzlich and Rachel Bagby and Elsa Menendez) has inspired me to appreciate diversity (or a full spectrum of perspectives and people) in *all* of its forms. Not only ethnic or racial diversity, but the real value of working among an array of ages, orientations, classes, abilities, faiths, disciplines and sectors. It has led me to a deeper understanding of the complementary values of extroversion and introversion, and how we all process information differently, applying visual, auditory and kinesthetic capacities and ways of learning in varied ways.

None of the women's leadership work of Bioneers has ever been about exclusion or reinforcing binaries. It has always been oriented toward balance and belonging, wholeness and integration. Some call it blended leadership, informed by a healthy integration of all of our feminine and masculine qualities. After twelve years of workshops with women, I've come to believe that leadership is more about finding the place where each of our unique gifts and talents connect with a real need for reinvention in the world. When we find that connection point, that nexus, we become unstoppable. The joy that is generated by doing the work creates a self-reinforcing loop. Once you find it, it's powerful and revitalizing, and defies those inherited definitions I had found so distasteful in myself.

I now believe that bringing the complete capacity of each of us — our own full-spectrum diversity — to our leadership might actually be the most appropriate, potent and useful response to this moment in time, when the world is asking so much of us. It has surprised me to notice how much energy, joy and creativity is unleashed within me as I reclaim my own greater inner wholeness.

As studying nature reveals, diversity is about far more than political correctness. It's actually about resilience and survival. In nature, diversity means having a plethora of options for adaptation in order to ensure survival and to mitigate against extinction. Ecosystems that are rich in diversity rebound much more quickly after trauma; systems with less species diversity are far slower to recover and heal. Since human systems are a subset of nature's systems, if diversity serves nature's resilience, well-being, and survival, it will serve ours as well.

What is needed in this pivotal time of ecological and social collapse is an uprising of this full-spectrum leadership in every one of us. A reclaiming of all our internal or personal parts into wholeness must also be mirrored by a full spectrum externally and politically — of engaged people across all sectors, disciplines, races, orientations, classes and ages who together are strengthened by the full capacity of our diversity, both inwardly and outwardly.

As you read these pages, I invite you to notice which parts of yourself that may have been previously hidden may be called forth, silenced or kept small. I hope you find this book — and the videos and podcasts referenced throughout — inspiring, expansive and heart-nourishing. Perhaps ideas or stories within it may enter your dreamtime, or inspire you to grow into or reclaim previously undervalued or banished parts of yourself.

I am honored and thankful to invite you to join me in this journey of exploration. To do so, I suggest that you first give yourself permission to fall in love. Fall in love with a place, with a people, with kids, a cause, an organization, a creature, anything that really lights you up. Then give yourself to it in some sort of purposeful action. You don't have to know what that means, exactly, or have it strategically mapped out in advance. You just have to commit to being its ally, to acting to defend or protect or improve its life. Then see who else is committed to it. Who is in this river you've opted to swim in, on behalf of our collective future?

I suggest bringing yourself to it with all the wisdom of your magnificent body, the knowing of your heart, your intellect, and your intuition. Call on all of your aspects, from your discipline and rigor to your compassion and empathy; from your strategic thinking and analysis to your body wisdom and instinctive feeling, from your masculine to your feminine, and everything in between. Bring all of yourself.

Lastly, I suggest that you trust that exactly who you are is what is needed at this moment in the world and that you are enough in every way to meet this assignment. Here's the best part: I'd suggest you do this not because it's right (though it is), not because it's needed (though it surely is), but because it is the most joyful, purposeful and fulfilling way to live your life.

Warmly,

Nina Simons

PART I

Cultivating
Inner Balance

MARRYING THE MOON
AND SUN WITHIN

SHIFTING GUIDANCE FROM HEAD TO HEART

All the brilliant, innovative and effective solutions and strategies
     won't be enough to shift our collective course
     without an accompanying — and radical — change of heart.

For me, what's central to alleviating humanity's strife
     and addressing the devastation we are wreaking upon our
     mother Earth
     is tending to an imbalance of the masculine and feminine.

Reclaiming the value of the feminine within each of us
     is essential to bringing our human wholeness
     to this time of revolutionary reinvention.

We have to practice loving, re-awakening and strengthening
     the feeling parts of ourselves:
     our intuition, our body wisdom,
     our dreams and our deep listening.

As we re-enliven the inner knowing of our hearts
     (understanding that relationships are far more important
     than accomplishments, goals or tasks),

we'll become better partners to ourselves,
    each other and the Earth.

If we practice our capacity to be comfortable
    with vulnerability, with uncertainty,
and with attending caringly to the cues and clues that surround us,
it will help us to re-synchronize with the world
        and become more resilient, flexible and adaptive to change.

This is not about devaluing the masculine side of ourselves;
it's about re-evaluating what a healthy masculine means.
It's about reclaiming the whole of our dimensional humanity.

For me, I find I must begin with my inner self,
since what I see out there likely reflects what's within me.
If I don't, it's far too easy (and not ultimately effective)
to blame others without cleaning, updating
      and reorienting my own operating system, first.

I am practicing re-sequencing my inner voices
so that my heart's instruction can lead,
and be supported by the plans, analysis,
      structures and strategies my mind creates.

      When I listen with my heart,
I am pierced with an empathic awareness
      that calls me into action beyond what any amount
of learning, reading or mental understanding can prompt.

I am stunned by the power of women, and our capacity to heal.
Wise elders, friends and mutual mentors
    among the women I am honored to work with
remind me to listen deeply to all my sources of guidance —
    to seek assistance from nature,
    from my dreams and intuition, to inquire of my ancestors,
    and listen for responses, before determining a course of action.

This requires me to peel away layers of patterning,
    of rushing to respond to prove my value through productivity.
It requires me to question old and deeply ingrained habits.

As I practice composting layers of acculturated learning
    that I absorbed unknowingly through the invisible
    water of culture we swim in,
I wonder whether I will ever be free of it.
I realize I need to decolonize my mind,
    and practice reclaiming and remembering
        other ways of knowing.

Along the way, I've discovered something about the feminine.
I'm learning that listening is not a passive act.
Life is teaching me that it doesn't just require my ears.
I'm learning to listen with my belly, my dreams and my intuition.

Not only does it require actively attending to receiving guidance,
I've discovered I also have to ask, in order to receive,
    and then wait — patiently if possible —
    for a response to come.

As I practice this —
with my inner self, with nature, with my body,
        with ancestors, and dreamtime and intuition —
I find I have many more sources of insight or guidance
than I'd previously imagined or remembered.

May we remember how to bring the wholeness of our humanity —
        our deep listening; our patient observation;
        our loving, powerful, tender hearts; our humble hands;
        and our prayers —
        to co-creating the conditions for thriving life.

A RIVER OF PURPOSE

A Human-Nature Landscape

If anyone had suggested to me as a youth that I might spend my thirties, forties and fifties co-creating an annual environmental conference serving a vision of restoration, I'd have said "No way!" In college, I always found biology and chemistry classes to be utterly boring and lacking any relevance for my life.

As a child growing up in New York City, however, nature provided comfort and sanctuary. When I was a girl of six or seven, I had a large and varied collection of stuffed animals that lived on my bed. One day, after my parents had read us *Charlotte's Web*, I piled them into shopping bags and took them to Central Park. There, I set each of them carefully into their own nook within a huge tree, returning them to nature, to be free among their own kind. I came home to an empty bed, happy with what I'd done.

Since that day, a strong sense of purpose has continued to grow and morph as new experiences and learning have shaped me. It's manifested as an evolving call, or assignment, and not something that remains static. In significant moments along the way, I have fallen in love, my heart and mind converging in newfound commitment to a people, a creature, a place or a challenge. And I have come to understand purpose as being what happens when one's own particular loves, commitments and talents converge with a need for change in the world. Those moments have shifted the course of my leadership, creating a long and windy river of expression, and not the direct and linear pathway I'd anticipated. As more of myself has become consciously engaged, bringing a full spectrum of my capacities into play, that has also informed how I've come to understand my purpose.

A daughter of artists, I assumed that it was through producing radical art that I'd make my contribution to the world. After college, I worked for a theater company, as I'd hoped to produce what I called transformational theater, theater that was capable of transforming people's hearts and minds. Discovering how hard it might be to earn a living that way, I managed restaurants and studied extensively with a school for consciousness called Arica.

In my late 20s, I moved to Santa Fe, New Mexico, and a few years later, I met Kenny Ausubel, who later became my husband and partner. It was early 1987, and he was completing a documentary film, *Hoxsey: How Healing Becomes a Crime*, which told the story of the politics of medicine and the history of alternative cancer therapies in this country. As I learned about the growing number of cancer patients and their lack of access to good information or options, I became passionate about addressing that gap, and helped him to complete, market and distribute the film.

Kenny has said that we came together like peanut butter and jelly, and it's true — our collaboration happened quite organically and seamlessly. We were so complementary that we finished each other's sentences and manifested each other's ideas, effortlessly. Working on distributing *Hoxsey* was a breakthrough experience for me in many ways. I learned that I loved helping get stories that are important for healing widely told. I found myself enthused and tireless in that pursuit, and strengthened by the synchronicity of my emerging partnership with Kenny.

A couple of years later, Kenny was asked to film footage of an
unusual garden at San Juan Pueblo near Santa Fe, New Mexico. He
went to visit the garden and became fascinated by the garden's diversity,
uniqueness and fertility. The pueblo had hired master gardener Gabriel
Howearth to design and plant the garden. Previously, Gabriel had
traveled all over Central and Latin America learning about Indigenous
agriculture, expanding his repertoire of diverse plant families. As people
began to trust him, they shared with him what for them was the most
precious of gifts — the gift of seeds.

At that time, I was working with the Santa Fe Chamber Music
Festival, but walking through Gabriel's garden changed the course of
my life. Strolling through it I encountered whole societies of tomatoes
and peppers, of every shape, size and color, and the smells were beyond
anything I'd ever experienced — totally intoxicating. There were tall
stalks of glowing red amaranth, golden braids of quinoa, and other
things that I had never seen before. As we walked, I was encouraged
to taste, so I picked leaves and munched my way through, feeling the
utter vitality of the whole environment coursing through my senses.
There was chocolate basil and lemon licorice mint. The richness and the
fertility of the garden resonated deeply within me, and I felt as though
my senses were dancing. Then, Gabriel told us of the impending crisis
in the food system. He shared how dozens of small seed companies
were being gobbled up by multinational corporations, diminishing the
number of varieties being grown and thereby threatening the diversity
of life itself. As we left the garden, I felt the spirit of the natural world
tap me on the shoulder and say, "You're working for me, now."

Kenny and Gabriel entered into a partnership to begin a
biodiversity seed company. I knew nothing about gardening, farming
or plant diversity and very little about the crisis in biodiversity. But I

did know that the life force I'd encountered in that garden had what
I saw as a thrilling capacity to renew and heal our world, and I threw
myself into the work fully. I quit my job and began working as Director
of Marketing for Seeds of Change, and while it was daunting to realize
how little I knew, it was exhilarating to work for something I believed
in so deeply. I found myself feeling more alive than with any work I'd
previously done.

In 1990, after bemoaning in a hot tub about all the amazing
innovators working to heal nature with nature that his research
was revealing, but that no one knew about, Kenny was offered a
grant by Josh Mailman to start a conference. Kenny had never been
to a conference, and wondered about it as a strategy, imagining
conferences as inherently boring. Knowing of my theater background,
he approached me to partner with him to produce a conference,
and Bioneers was born. Since neither of us had ever experienced a
conventional conference, we were able to design something with
beginner's mind, and we co-created a form that could simultaneously
integrate a sense of the sacred with ceremony, that could speak to the
heart and imagination with arts and culture, and bring brilliant and
largely unknown ideas and people to light.

I embarked on three steep and deep learning curves — one
about food and farming, another about being a social entrepreneur,
and the third about leadership. Those inquiries led me into a lifelong
exploration of Indigenous wisdom, and how to interact, design, invent,
educate and organize on behalf of the sacred web of life on Earth.

When I first heard the speakers that Kenny invited at that initial
Bioneers conference in 1990, my jaw dropped. Science came alive for
me for the first time, and I felt my childlike sense of wonder return.
Here were courageous and curious explorers whose experiments with

natural systems were revealing the complexity and brilliance of 4 billion years of evolution. Contrary to the arrogant and mechanistic way I'd previously experienced science, here were people quivering with the delight of discovery, humbly studying at the feet of a real master — nature herself.

It was at Bioneers, too, through Kenny's commitment to Indigenous voices and values, that I first heard Native American people speak about healing from an Indigenous perspective — one that included greater relatedness to place, to each other, to the Earth and all its creatures. Hearing them, I understood that their knowledge and experience were essential to our survival as a species. Having already adapted to thousands of years of change, Indigenous peoples have information about how we are meant to live that I believe must be reintegrated in order to reinvent our entire culture.

At the 1992 Bioneers Conference, to commemorate Columbus's tragic landing on Turtle Island, we assembled a group of Indigenous leaders to discuss what could be learned from considering this 500th anniversary. A man from Acoma Pueblo, Petuuche Gilbert, said, "Five hundred years ago you came, and we welcomed you with open arms. If you came again today, we would do exactly the same." I was humbled, awed and shaken by his words. I sensed how much wisdom his culture carried about forgiveness and generosity, about how to be a good person, as well as about survival. Many native growers knew about dryland agriculture, about seed breeding for resilience and nutrition, about how to live in reciprocal relationship with nature. Relating to all life as sacred seems just about endemic to Indigeneity.

My days were on fire with learning and producing and convening, but it wasn't until a few years later that my path took another unexpected turn, when I began exploring my identity as a woman. I had always assumed, coming out of college, that I was stepping onto a relatively level playing field thanks to the hard work of the feminists of the 60s and 70s. It wasn't until I was working in my thirties that I began to realize how untrue that assumption had been. I had the repeated experience of sitting in a board room, saying something, and having it fall on deaf ears, and then the man next to me would say it with slightly different language and everybody would nod their heads, saying, "What a great idea." I began to understand how bifurcated and unconsciously biased I, like our whole society, still was around issues of gender.

One day, after we'd left Seeds of Change and my father had suddenly died, I went into a favorite video shop seeking a film to rent, hoping for solace, or to fill some of the void I was feeling. Carmen Blue, the woman who ran the store, said, "I've got a film for you. I feel it's so important for everyone to see that I lend it out to people for free." She handed me *The Burning Times*, which is an hour-long documentary now viewable for free online. The film changed the course of my life.

When I learned about the period in European history between the 14th and 17th centuries — a time many refer to as *The Burning Times* — my mind and heart's eyes were opened to a root cause of centuries of pervasive gender patterns and biases. I marveled that this immense event in human history wasn't being taught to every child in school.

I discovered that seven generations of children across Europe saw many of their mothers, grandmothers, aunties and sisters tortured and burned for the supposed crime of being witches. Men, too, lost loved ones — wives, daughters, local healers. To save their families and themselves, women were often turned against each other.

The culture also sustained deep institutional losses that further cemented structural biases. Traditional systems of healing, spiritual practice, communal land use and economic relationships were upended, as power was systematically transferred from the collective purview of women in these domains to the primary control, authority and leadership of men. What some have called "The Hidden Holocaust of Women" lives on in my cellular memory, and I believe still insidiously permeates our society, institutions and collective psyche.

It was also the first time an irrational fear I'd always had of speaking my truth in public made sense to me. At this point, all of the issues I'd become passionate about through Bioneers began to come into focus *within a single lens*: the imbalance of "masculine" values and a patriarchal relationship to competition, hierarchy and power over "feminine" values: cooperation, shared authority, and the equity of women. I saw this as evident both externally, in the disproportionate allotment of leadership roles to men in nearly all spheres of life, and internally, as an archetypal inner imbalance that affects the design and functioning of every individual, institution and sector.

I began a deep inquiry about the role of gender in my own life and realized that I carried stories within me that were self-limiting. I observed how long I'd held myself back due to unexplored fears and unconsciously adopted stories. For example, once I was asked to write the story of my relationship to Bioneers, the organization that I co-midwifed and co-shepherded into being. I wrote that my role consisted of supporting my husband's vision, and then I wondered, "Ugh, is that the whole truth?" What I found was that other people around me, including my husband, didn't see this story as true at all. They perceived its evolution as co-created, and they frequently valued my contributions more than I valued my own.

Along with many other self-limiting beliefs that I had
unconsciously absorbed, I recognized that I was relying upon
these stories to make myself small. And the gift in that, of course,
was realizing that if I had let those stories shape my thoughts or
constrain my dreams, I could, now that they were exposed to the
light, let them go, or at least re-craft them. Much of my work
on myself since then has been to do that. As I shared my own
discoveries with other women around me, I saw everyone nodding
their heads. Then I realized, "This isn't just me; this is a rather
pervasive pattern held by many women, a pattern that must be
illuminated so it can transform."

As I investigated my inner landscape, I realized that I had
lived much of my outer life through my more "masculine" qualities
— showing up as competent, self-assured, intelligent, decisive, linear
and rational, while my more "feminine" aspects — my intuition,
relational intelligence, embodied awareness, empathy, flexibility and
a tendency toward a chaotic process of creativity — I tended to keep
hidden and rarely revealed in a public context. Of course, I knew
that we all have feminine and masculine aspects within us, but when
I saw this imbalance within myself, I wanted to claim more of my
human wholeness. I began to practice valuing my more "feminine"
aspects, exploring how I might express them more fully in my work,
relationships and everyday life.

At the 2001 Bioneers conference, a remarkable activist
named Diane Wilson closed her speech by adopting a quote from
George Bernard Shaw. She said, "A reasonable woman adapts to the
world, and an unreasonable woman makes the world adapt to her.
So, I encourage all of you women out there to be unreasonable."
After the conference, she called Kenny and me at home and told

us how so many women had thanked her, tearfully, for what she'd said, and that she'd had a vision that there would be a movement of unreasonable women.

With Kenny's encouragement, I decided that I would help seed this vision by bringing together a diverse group of women leaders to explore what such a movement might look like. I expanded the title of the gathering — as I knew that resistance wasn't enough, and we had to be *for* something — to "UnReasonable Women for the Earth." I invited 34 women ranging in age from 23 to 70 years old, from across many disciplines, social classes, gender orientations and ethnicities. They worked in domains as varied as environmental health, law, poetry, social organizing, performance art, writing, seed diversity, urban farming, spiritual teaching and science.

When we first arrived at the meeting, each spoke about her own feelings of isolation, and we recognized that we each had a need for a community of peers. By the end of the four days, a solidarity developed among us — a pledge to stand at each other's backs — that nourished us in unexpected ways.

One thing that grew out of that gathering was the emergence of CODEPINK: Women for Peace. Jodie Evans, Medea Benjamin and Diane Wilson, inspired by the visions at the retreat, and prompted by the urgency of that time and their resistance to the U.S. invasion and war in Iraq, founded CODEPINK several months later.

We had been programming diverse women's voices in leadership at the Bioneers Conference for several years, and had also explored the theme of what I called "Restoring the Feminine." Our radio series had also been featuring shows each year that explored and helped promote multicultural women's voices, visions and perspectives, but I wanted to go deeper.

I wanted to explore how women can come together and
strengthen each other. We had experienced conventional forms
of leadership, based upon hierarchy and competition rather than
relationship, and power rather than respect, for 6,000 years. It had left
our world in dire shape. The time had come to model the respectful,
relational connectivity that we know as a true pattern of life and stand
up for that option to emerge among women leading change. And so in
2006 I reached out first to Toby Herzlich and then Akaya Windwood, a
couple of very skillful facilitators of group transformative processes, and
together we three co-created a six-day, deep-dive immersion training
into leading from the feminine, which was incubated and housed
as a program within Bioneers. We named it "Cultivating Women's
Leadership" (CWL).

During these six-day residential trainings we prioritized probing
what leadership meant to women. We focused on exploring how it
differed from conventional male models and investigated how we
might more wholeheartedly claim leadership and aspire to it. Through
experiential learning, we encouraged the women who were participating
to identify and overcome internalized limitations and to face and
acknowledge the shadow side of women's leadership. We developed
exercises to help clarify each woman's purpose in life, and to learn how
powerfully women in intentional alignment can strengthen each other's
capacity. Toby and I, as the primary cofounders, have produced CWL
trainings each year since 2006. Each cohort of twenty women was
caringly selected (through an application process) for their leadership
vision and capacity, and we also sought to optimize diversity in all its
forms among each group.

This group process included many aspects; it was intentionally
highly multi-dimensional, but for me, a highlight has been that

it's revealed how we as women have the capacity to rapidly and exponentially enhance each other's skillfulness and to stand at each other's backs. Once the women hear and see each other's visions and gifts and power, they become committed to supporting each other. Everyone who comes has an opportunity to do her own deep inquiry and to explore fundamental questions: What is calling me? How can I refine my sense of assignment or purpose? One of our core premises is that each of us has a very distinct, unique purpose/reason for being alive on Earth at this momentous time.

In recent years, co-facilitating while continually improving the program with co-founder Toby Herzlich, and the remarkably gifted Rachel Bagby and Elsa Menendez, we've been adding skill-building around freeing women's voices, awakening body awareness and sense of play, and dealing with relational ruptures that occur around power and privilege.

We discovered that in order to feel comfortable enough to fully express themselves, members of any minority group need to have at least 30 percent representation, so we established that minimum for women of color in our trainings, and since then often attract 35–50 percent. About five hundred women leaders, across a huge span of ages, disciplines, races, backgrounds and orientations, from the U.S. and around the world, have now been through CWL. A vast majority of them report that they were profoundly changed by the experience.

As my understanding grew, I sought to identify patterns among the leaders I'd most admired throughout my years with Bioneers. In 2010, Anneke Campbell and I edited an anthology called *Moonrise: The Power of Women Leading from the Heart*. We collected the stories by reading scores of transcripts, and in spite of the publisher's protests, we realized that we wanted to include the stories of some men who also embodied relationship intelligence and leading from the heart. I think of the book as an homage to my mentors, as everyone profiled in the book has inspired me deeply with the way they've modeled innovative and effective forms of leadership. The book is being used in colleges as part of the curriculum for Women's Studies, Leadership & Social Change, and Multiculturalism classes, in addition to, of course, being read by individuals and shared in book clubs and other organizations.

Seeing the need for some larger organizing principle to build power among diverse factions of women's movements, in 2014 I began convening diverse women leaders of networks and organizations to explore their interest and availability in creating such a connective tissue. These gatherings were called "Comadres," borrowing from the Chicana term for women who've pledged to have each other's backs, for life. Although they have been relatively small and intimate, they have been effective at seeding key relationships. Through that work, and CWL and Bioneers, I've formed some deep friendships with women from many different cultures. The more I got to know and heard people of all colors and classes speak, the more I understood the degree to which our culture operates in a hierarchical paradigm that tends to devalue people of color, people of lower income, and ultimately women as well.

I guess I must have been naïve, but what I learned about our racialized culture and the ways it impacts people I love shocked me and woke me up. Experiencing it personally through friends I'd come to know helped me to understand that if I had felt limited, oppressed or constrained because of my gender identity as a woman, it was minimal compared to the experiences of the Indigenous women and women of color I was coming to know. They typically had many of the internalized oppression and self-limiting beliefs that come with gender in our culture, but they also had had to face the intense

NATURE, CULTURE AND THE SACRED   33

constraints a racist social order and colonization places on people of color, a double whammy.

I began to learn more directly about the physical impacts of living in those African American, Indigenous and Latino communities that suffer the worst toxic health threats and the toxic psychic and psychological impacts of current and intergenerational trauma. This began to radicalize me, and awakened within me a far more visceral understanding of the depth of the injustices racism has wrought.

What shocked me most was coming to see my own prior ignorance, denial and complicity. Over time I began to challenge myself to compare the experiences all women have had of gender bias with that of racial bias. I have to admit that exploring these charged topics has been unsettling and has stirred up a lot of deep fears I'd not previously known I carried within me.

As painful as it is, facing these fears is something we all have to do in order to realize the dream of building sustainable multicultural and cross-class alliances. I've tried to continue learning from women of color, and as they shared their stories, I began to feel in my gut the insidious, pervasive costs of white privilege we all ultimately pay for, and how those deep wounds are compounded by how we are all programmed around gender. I'm still working to shed my own blinders, ignorance, guilt and shame, something I'll have to continue to do for the rest of my days, but I'm slowly learning, and I'm now able to recover sooner when I make mistakes or find I've made false assumptions.

I am also finding it helpful to explore my own Jewish heritage, to relate to my own lineage with dignity and respect and gratitude for what it can offer me. In this way, I can bring my own culture with me into relationship, and not just behave as if I don't have roots, though, of course, Jewish culture has been uprooted repeatedly throughout its long history as well. Perhaps we are a people who've learned over thousands of years of displacement how to carry culture on our backs, like turtles carry their shells.

If you had told me ten years before that my interest in the arts, healing and leadership would lead to this, I would have been shocked. It was never in my game plan or vision for myself but following the path of what I most cared about led me there, organically, and I am deeply thankful for it. My life continues to be an unpredictable and winding road, and I'm finally making peace with that aspect of my true nature.

A theme that has come up frequently at Bioneers over the decades is that in nature the systems with the greatest biodiversity are the ones that are most resilient and most capable of rebounding after trauma. Our human systems are exactly the same. Therefore, well beyond tolerating diversity and valuing it, I am committed to a future where we celebrate and recognize how essential our human diversity is toward regenerating our relationship with ourselves, each other and the Earth. We've inherited deep relational imbalances in those three fundamental relationships. They are interdependent and interrelated, and all need to be healed for the system to be transformed.

The issue of climate justice has also emerged as a central focus for me. I have found that the movement emerging to address it encompasses so many of the things I have cared most deeply about in my life: art, healing, biodiversity, environmental justice, Indigenous wisdom, women's leadership and racial justice. My heart is now calling me to find new ways to engage with some aspects of that movement's framing and organizing, and supporting frontline leaders in the struggle, especially the Indigenous ones, in defense of our mother Earth.

Through this twenty-year, multifaceted engagement with women's leadership and the feminine, I have come to see how these fractal, yet mutually dependent issues are essential to us all — individually and collectively — in order to unearth, explore and reframe our narratives as we navigate this immense systemic transition we face. If we're humble, persevering and honoring of the wisdom that's all around us, respecting the true value of the feminine to bring new life, and guided by our hearts, intuitions, dreams, ancestors and bodies, as well as our minds, we may just find our way through.

LISTENING FOR GUIDANCE

Mystery, Intuition and Dreamtime

I learned in an embodied way about the power of dreams and of listening for guidance from the mystery to inform leadership through a lived experience of Indigenous wisdom. Called the Four Societies process (when translated into English), it is an ancient way of bringing a group of diverse people into alignment — what I sometimes refer to as a transformative practice, or what some call a "social technology." Here is a story of what happened that describes both the unanticipated, intuitive and sacred way that guidance was received among a group, and that also provides a model of servant leadership that I've found useful and inspiring.

Years ago, Bioneers hosted a retreat led in a traditional way by Jeannette Armstrong and Marlowe Sam, educators from the Okanagan people, some of the First Peoples of what is now called British Columbia and Washington State. One of the things that we learned during this retreat was to listen for the mystery — the sacred information that comes, unbidden. Each night they gave us a topic to explore in a dream and asked us to report back to the group the next day.

On the last morning of a six-day immersion, we'd been asked to dream about the future of Bioneers. In my dream, I'd seen a turtle and a long furry creature I'd never seen before frolicking together, in and out of underwater caves. The tone of the dream was playful and celebratory, and I awoke feeling happy and refreshed.

Having no idea what it meant, I brought it to Jeannette over breakfast, knowing her to be a skilled dream interpreter. After listening intently, she assured me that I'd understand later, when the group gathered. In the circle, we shared our dreams, and several others had dreamt about turtles, too.

Then, Marlowe described his dream. A large shed-like building was on a beach, with a long line of people going in one end and coming out the other. In the center of the shed was a mound of sand, with a hole at its center. Out of it poured a steady stream of newly hatched baby sea turtles. As each person approached the mound, they'd pick up a baby turtle and carry it tenderly away to care for its survival. Now our circle was very still, all of us utterly silent, as we were held in the conjoined mystical web of our dreams.

Next, Jeannette told us an origin story that's been told to children as a teaching story among the Okanagan people for generations. This was also approved by their Elders to be told as an educational story for all people.

One day, she said, the Creator gathered all the creatures together for a meeting. Once assembled, Creator told them, *"Soon, there will come among you new beings who will not be as intelligent as you are. Once they come, they will need to be shown how to institute stability. You will need to determine which way would work best for them."*

There was much discussion among the animals, as they were uncertain what might work best. Then, Eagle stepped forward, saying, *"I propose that I decide for all of you, since I am strong and fast, and can see a long, long way. I should decide everything, unless any of you are stronger or faster than me. The only way to find out if anyone else is faster is if you can beat me in a race. If you can't beat me, then you have to do everything I say."*

Since nobody else had any ideas, this seemed reasonable, and so they all agreed. One by one, the animals challenged Eagle to a race. But Eagle was very fast, and each time, he won. Finally, there seemed to be nobody left to race, and Eagle became the leader of all the creatures. But as soon as he did, he began changing how all the animals spent their days. He ordered them to build nests for his children, to hunt for them and feed them.

In order to do all that Eagle asked of them, they had to ignore the needs of their own families and their own children. They became thin and hungry. The animals became more and more dejected as they became enslaved to Eagle. Their children were suffering. The land was neglected. With each new race that was lost to Eagle, their spirits sank lower and lower. They didn't see how they could ever reclaim their freedom and restore their community.

About that time, Turtle emerged out of the river and learned what was going on. He was deeply concerned for all the others. He saw their suffering, and he felt compelled to act. He had no idea how he could help free them and restore peace and balance to the land, but he knew he must do his best.

He challenged Eagle to a race. When Eagle learned of Turtle's challenge, he laughed scornfully. Turtle was known to be the slowest animal of all. Eagle said to everyone listening,

"I'll let Turtle pick the time, the place and set the length of the race. If Turtle wins, he can decide for everyone, even the people-to-be."

Turtle said *"We will race in the morning, after I rest. We will meet here at this big tree where everything began, and then I will let you know where and how long the race will be."*

Turtle went down into the river and prayed for help. He didn't know how he could possibly remedy the situation, but he desperately hoped he'd be able to find a way.

During that night Turtle was given a dream. In the morning the animals all gathered around the base of the big tree to witness the race. Though they were despondent, tired and discouraged, a few still had a tiny gleam of hope in their eyes.

Turtle walked up, and Eagle condescendingly inquired where Turtle would like the race to begin. Turtle replied that he would like to race from the top of that same tree, and asked Eagle to give him a ride on his back, and when they reached the top, to deposit him there. Eagle agreed, and flew Turtle to the top of the tree.

When the race started — a race to the ground — Turtle pulled in his arms, legs, head and tail, and dropped like a stone. Eagle tried his best, folding his wings in and diving down head first, but he was no match for Turtle. Turtle was fearless, plummeting straight down and hit the ground first, beating Eagle!

The animals were overjoyed and let out a tremendous cheer for Turtle. Turtle had landed with a thwack on his hard back, jarring him badly, and he lay there, stunned and seeing stars.

His friend Muskrat came to tend him, saying *"Are you all right? You've won, and released all the animals from the tyranny of Eagle! Now, what will you decide for all of us?"*

Turtle arose and happily told all the animals that all living beings would now be free to live their own lives, building nests for their young, finding food for their families, caring for their own places, and keeping balance in the world.

In the future, he said, the people-to-be were to learn to do the same. All the animals rejoiced (except for Eagle) and Turtle and Muskrat returned to the river that was their home.

I was stunned by my dream's relationship to the story, so vividly reflecting the end of the tale. Turtle knew why he had to act, though he didn't know how. His rational mind offered no clues. His determination, caring and perseverance were undaunted. He sought counsel, and listened — until his way became clear.

This is the inquiry: What is the particular talent within each of us, as unique and unlikely as Turtle's, that might be the unforeseen gift that could help free the world?

May we too learn to embrace all our ways of knowing — listening for the wisdom of body, heart, intuition and mind. May we tend fully to our relational intelligence, so that we might re-nourish the soil and regrow our roots to form an underground web of connection with each other, like aspen trees do — to help anchor us for the coming storms.

CULTIVATING RELATIONAL INTELLIGENCE

What lies at the heart of many of the toughest issues that we face, both as a culture and as a species? As crucial as they are to illuminate a future landscape of hope, innovative environmental solutions and strategic social models alone won't be enough to alter our collective course. What's ultimately required is a change of heart, a shift in how we relate to each other and to the whole of the living Earth. The root source of our gravest challenges — both socially and environmentally — is a crisis of relationship.

The tear in our relational fabric is apparent in every area of our lives. The evidence surrounds us — from the corporate invasion of our schools to the profusion of divorce and domestic violence; from toxic factory farming to the loss of civil liberties; and from deforestation and global warming to people making war on each other all over the world. We've got a lot to learn about how to be in relationship in a way that is not only enduring, but can help us to heal our personal and societal wounds.

In times of drastic change, the social philosopher Eric Hoffer said: "It is the learners who inherit the future. The learned usually find themselves equipped to live in a world that no longer exists." How, then, can we enhance and accelerate our learning about cultivating conscious kinship?

First, it might help to stop idolizing rational intelligence to the exclusion of our other capacities to relate to the living world. As the biologist Candace Pert noted: "We have bodies for other reasons than to transport our heads around." A wealth of additional information might be available to us, if we also valued the abundant physical, emotional and intuitive cues we receive. Western culture has long over-emphasized the importance of rational intelligence or IQ.

Unfortunately for most of us, reorienting ourselves toward a broader focus that integrates emotional or relational intelligence means swimming against the tide. For many centuries throughout our history the value of emotional feeling, sensing and other relationship skills have been vastly underrated, derided or even scorned. Most often they have been relegated to the disrespected world of "intuition" or sentimentality, and ascribed mostly to the women, children and elderly. Our other ways of knowing, through our hearts, hands and spirits, have become weakened from disuse and often internally discounted, especially by ourselves.

How then can we reorient ourselves to reclaim those attributes, to be better able to bring a full spectrum of our capacities into play to become more adept at navigating and sustaining respectful relationships? Into play, not only with each other, but also with ourselves and with the sacred and diverse community of life upon which we all depend?

"The real voyage of discovery," Marcel Proust wrote, "lies not in seeking new landscapes, but in having new eyes." To have "new eyes" to seek a deeper understanding of what it means to become more fully human, let us look to the biology of love. Ultimately, I believe, there is nothing with as big a capacity as love to turn our collective path towards one that is life-affirming, and to reweave wholeness into our tattered social fabric.

What do we really know about the current state of relationship and how it manifests among our families, organizations and institutions? We live in a culture that cultivates despair instead of joy, numbness in lieu of feeling, and separation in place of intimacy; a culture that seems to believe that the domination of mind over feeling is our civilization's crowning glory and that material gain is more important than emotional fulfillment. While romance novels and bridal magazines flourish, divorce rates remain staggeringly high. In our educational system, children are taught to memorize facts, equations and theorems but not how to cultivate and retain friendships, respect each other's perspectives, or navigate the demands and challenges of intimacy. In business and governance, historically the brightest, most powerful debaters or strategists have held sway, though that's beginning to change.

However, this is not a contest between head and heart — that peace treaty is long overdue. The most encouraging news is that our capacity to love is something we can learn.

A collaboration among three San Francisco Bay Area professors — Thomas Lewis, Fari Amini and Richard Lannon — resulted in a remarkable book, *A General Theory of Love*. This team combed the neuro-scientific literature, seeking to learn how to map human relationships, hoping to learn about the biology of love. As science has begun, only recently, to explore the brain's mysteries, some surprising insights are emerging.

Their research suggests that it is the supremely complex activity of the one hundred billion neurons of the human brain and the pathways they form — all working together in a collaborative way — that determine the nature of love. The brain is actually comprised of three distinct sub-brains, each with a very different function and chemistry. The oldest brain, sometimes popularly called the "reptilian" brain, is the innermost brain — a bulbous extension of the spinal cord.

It is the one most directly responsible, physiologically, for our survival — it regulates our breathing, swallowing and heartbeat, and also prompts our swift reaction to an abrupt movement or loud noise. It is the only brain that reptiles are known to have, and emotionality is not in its repertoire.

The brain that's wrapped around it, that is unique to mammals like us, developed about a hundred million years ago. It is called the limbic brain. In addition to having different ways than reptiles of bearing our young, we relate to our young differently by integrating nurturing communication that plays into the relationship, while reptiles often exhibit disinterest or even sometimes cannibalism in interacting with their young.

The most recently developed brain, the neocortex, provides us with our capacity for problem-solving. Speaking, writing, planning and reasoning all stem from the neocortex, as do the experience of our senses and our conscious motor control, what we sense as our capacity to reason and our "will."

Problem-solving is a wonderful thing and is part of what we at Bioneers celebrate, but we seem to have gone a bit overboard on the neocortex express. We now undervalue emotions, since our culture, in the authors' words, "promotes analysis over intuition, logic above feeling. And, as it exalts reason, this nation buries its emotions …" — a practice that currently results in, among other things, the largest use of mood-altering drugs in the history of humankind. Our elevated reverence for the intellect — the reason of the neocortex — has led us to a state of relational illiteracy, of impoverished heart-centered passion and compassion.

Albert Einstein famously noted: "We should take care not to make the intellect our god: it has, of course, powerful muscles, but no personality. It cannot lead; it can only serve."

Our limbic system, which houses our physical repertoire for emotional relationship, develops in a reciprocal loop with our parents, and later with others. As parents are attentive, providing mirroring, feedback and responsiveness, the physical architecture of relatedness is built structurally into a child's neural system. As a child matures, its limbic resonance becomes more autonomous, but it is still developed, strengthened like a muscle, from emotional exchanges with others — peers, friends and lovers.

All healthy people, regardless of age, require shared intimacy to be whole and healthy. Essential in defining who we are, our neural architecture places loving relationships at the very center of our lives, where — alive, generative and warm — they have the power to stabilize our very nature. Not having an attuned mother is an utter nonevent — perhaps even a blessing — for a reptile, but for a mammal, it is a shattering injury to the fragile and complex limbic brain. For people, neural patterning happens early in life, and then tends to reinforce itself. For those of us who have had a traumatic early childhood, without a course correction, we are wired to repeat the same emotional experiences we've grown up to expect.

Many of those who grew up with neglect or abuse, whose lives have been punctuated with loss, abandonment and rage, have one thing in common: a profound, lifelong familiarity with the pain of separation.

The sense of prolonged separation or relationship rupture is a huge physical strain for any mammal to endure, as it causes us to produce dramatically higher rates of cortisol, the body's major stress hormone.

The stability that intimate relationships provide also impacts both our individual and societal capacity for discernment. As the authors note: "When a society loses touch with limbic bedrock, spin wins."

The great good news is this: limbic connections can still be grown, even after a childhood of abuse and neglect. The capacity for love cannot be grown through any amount of reasoning or will, but warm human contact can trigger the release of pleasure-inducing neurohormonal secretions in the brain, a feel-good sensation that is potent magic indeed. Developing a living relationship is a form of therapy that takes time; it's not adapted to the "quick fix" orientation of our culture. Rebuilding neural pathways requires that the formerly traumatized person find enduring care, appreciation and love in others.

Sustaining a relationship demands care, attention and sensory inputs that are visceral, vivid, recurring and frequent. In a relationship, we can change each other, depending upon the strength of our limbic connection. The encouraging revelation of our mammalian legacy is this capacity for limbic revision: the ability to change and expand the people we love, emotionally. In this way who we are and who we become is dependent — in large part — on whom we love. And, as Dr. Martin Luther King, Jr. put it: "Along the way of life, someone must have sense enough and morality enough to cut off the chain of hate. This can only be done by projecting the ethic of love to the center of our lives, since love is mankind's most potent weapon for personal and social transformation."

In witnessing the lifeways, cultures and practices of most Indigenous peoples, we are reminded that they strengthen their relationships to the Earth and all the elements of life through dances, ceremonies and rituals that reinforce those connections regularly. In the evolution of lifelong couples or friends, they often testify to the ways they have healed each other's prior wounds, and grown each other. Children raised in Waldorf schools have stronger relationships to their own creativity and inner lives, and in turn to others, as a result of that system's emphasis on growing the whole person. Youth who experience trainings in nature and school gardens are often more sensitized to their relational skills than those who've only experienced urban realities. The rapid growth of mindfulness and other meditation practices that cultivate the mind's stillness and value deep listening are improving people's capacity to accept what is, and to receive guidance. These alternative ways of living and relating, emerging and proliferating throughout the world, are among the most hopeful realities we've got to build on.

A more relational orientation is peeking over the horizon in a wide range of domains and disciplines. Increasingly, research is revealing the value of whole-body learning, proving that our entire neural networks and our emotions are profoundly involved in all thought and in how we relate to the world and create meaning.

New communications disciplines can offer a helpful framework through which to revisit and develop our "relational musculature." The emerging field of nonviolent communication, for example, suggests that in situations of conflict we track the emotions that lie beneath the content of the words. By responding receptively to the emotional message — and not the verbal or mental one — embattled moments can become swiftly defused, creating a real opening for people to question their previous positions and reach resolution.

Promising relational social technologies are emerging in many fields. Thanks in large part to the late Candace Pert's work on the "molecules of emotion," the study of emotional intelligence, or EQ, is expanding rapidly. People who have a higher "EQ" tend to have happier, more productive and fulfilling lives. EQ is defined as "the ability to perceive emotions, to access and generate emotions to assist thought, to understand emotions, and to reflectively regulate emotions so as to promote emotional and intellectual growth."

Cultivating our capacity to step outside of our emotional
reactions and noting them more dispassionately might offer the time
and space needed to assess a number of possible responses, in order
to select the one that's most relationally attuned. With a history of
relations that have reinforced hierarchy, domination and disrespect as
the norm, we have a lot of unlearning to do. To alter our orientation
to one of partnership, collaboration and reciprocity will require real
commitment, practice and patience.

As products of a culture that has prized individualism and
separation, this is far easier said than done. Ask anyone who's been in a
long-term relationship. Based on my own relationship, which is blessed
with both co-creativity and shared vision, I can honestly say it's the
hardest spiritual work I know…and the most rewarding. When we seem
to hit an impasse, or a place where we vehemently disagree, if I can step
back from my reactive response, drop into my heart, and focus on my
willingness to alter my perspective instead of my need to be right, the
story changes and we may again find common ground.

But I believe that our biological orientation toward
relationship, and what biologist E.O. Wilson calls *biophilia* — that
innate affinity that life has for life — strengthens our likelihood
of success. As human beings, we're built for relationship. Our
young remain dependent far longer than most other creatures, and
our neural systems and limbic brains are hardwired for empathy,
compassion and connection. We're a highly adaptable species, and one
of our finest adaptive strategies is as mimics.

Fortunately, we have an abundance of relational intelligence
to learn from, if only we can humbly accept its tutelage. The
natural world is resplendent with symbiotic, long-term, reciprocal
relationships: between blossom and pollinator, moisture and

mycelium, plants and herbivores. In nature, no one lives in isolation, and the sense of balanced interdependence is palpable in any thriving ecosystem. If we can quiet ourselves long enough to listen, smell, feel and learn from nature, our survival as well as our joy may depend on our making this shift to bringing a practice of relational learning to the center of our attention.

In the Cherokee language there's no word for the love of an inanimate thing; love is only possible between two sentient beings. Anyone who loves a thing is considered insane, and, both personally and politically, we've paid a very high price for the commodification of nearly everything in our culture; for, as Jeremy Rifkin says, "valuing belongings more than belonging." Fortunately, there are some encouraging signs of change on levels ranging from the personal to the societal.

We have inherited a false separation between our minds and hearts, which are in fact utterly and interdependently linked. As the renowned Chilean biologist and neuroscientist Humberto Maturana wrote: "Love, allowing the other to be a legitimate other, is the only emotion that expands intelligence."

This is my prayer for us in this pivotal time. May we all attend to reuniting our heads, hearts and hands, taking some time to be receptive, suspend judgment and wait patiently for the information that arrives, unbidden. May we practice being still and really listening — to ourselves, to each other and to the gentle whispers of the living intelligences of the natural world.

To navigate the wild changes ahead to decrease the violence of this tumultuous time and shift our civilization's direction, we will need to invest the same authority and value in our relational intelligence and learning as we've previously given to our intellectual development. If we can do that, we will build a contagious energy that will ultimately lead to real healing and restoration — the restoration of our wholeness as a global community. That evolution may lead to the celebration and flourishing of our deep and fundamental interdependence with each other, other species and the whole interwoven web of creation.

As the Lakota people say, in ending every prayer: *Omatakeosin* — to All Our Relations.

THROUGH DARKNESS,
AND INTO VISION

I n the darkest, quietest time of year, I was fortunate to experience a
retreat called a Winter Dreaming Ceremony. When I learned of the
chance to be in the redwoods in the depth of winter, to journey deep
inside my own experience in a gentle, skillful and loving way, all the
cells of my body said "yes."

There, in sync with the Earth's cycle of hibernation and
dreaming, I discovered — or perhaps I remembered — the dimensional
creativity and fullness of darkness.

We lay on mats, covered in blankets, deep inside a darkened,
womb-like space. In silence, in pitch blackness, eyes open, we
practiced "receiving" for several hours, doing nothing but listening
and observing with our bodies, our inner sight, and our intuition.

To my surprise, I learned that my notion that darkness
might be devoid of substance was utterly unfounded. I discovered
that darkness is profoundly peaceful, abundant and creative, and
that turning inward to vision in the depths of winter is exactly what
this animal yearns for and is designed to do.

I found that vision can be what you see in the dark.

In my work with women leaders, I've seen how powerfully
we can see, hear and reflect each other into flourishing, that often
the act of seeing another's full magnificence and reflecting it to her
honestly can help her more fully see herself.

As a facilitator, I have learned the value of active listening, and I have discovered that more of me can be useful in inviting others to realize their own greatness. I have realized that we call each other into fullness — into healing and strength and greater leadership with our eyes, with our dreams and intuition, and with the insight of our inner vision.

One spring a few years ago, I began to notice that my eyesight was getting worse. An MRI revealed a tumor behind my right eye that was rapidly diminishing my sight, as it was wrapped around my optic nerve.

Tests revealed a startling truth — that my right eye wasn't able to perceive color.

A young doctor interpreted my situation and frightened me to the core. He said I'd need surgery very soon, and that there was a danger that I might lose my right eye's vision completely. The most common approach involved drilling a hole in my skull for the surgeons to be able to biopsy the tumor.

I drove home, deeply shaken, and shared my news with Kenny. We spent the night worrying, tossing and turning, and I awoke pre-dawn, in darkness. The first thing I heard was a soft rain spattering on our roof, which is rare at night and always evokes joy and gratitude in the desert.

Next, I realized that Kenny was sitting on the edge of our bed, his head in his hands, weeping.

I reached for him, and we held each other, riding a pure wave of emotion in our love, shock and dread. I was thankful for how we were together and for the mutual expression of our love, after weathering the twists and turns that come with any long marriage.

Then, the sun broke over the horizon. As I watched, a huge rainbow spread brilliantly across the sky. The moment was crystalline, magic and filled with a sacredness I have come to know as Gaia, or Mother Life. I knew that I would somehow make it through this journey.

Some weeks later, I had the least-invasive, most-successful surgery I could possibly have wished for. Mysterious grace, relationship and synchronicity led me to find the optimal doctors for my treatment, who used endoscopic technologies guided by a camera, and with exquisite care were able to successfully remove the tumor through my nose, without any external wounding.

Though my optic nerve had been damaged, which meant that my right eye's vision might not fully recover, they assured me that over time it would largely return.

Returning home, I embarked upon a journey of healing, learning to become an expert on my body's own needs. Since this strange science fiction surgery I'd received left me with no visible scars, this became a very intimate, interior endeavor. It asked me to focus all my vision inwardly, to listen intently to address the invisible bruising, aching and inflammation.

My color vision returned, gradually but incrementally, subtly and slowly.

Time has become essential to my healing and the reclaiming of my vision. I surrendered to my body's own pacing and needs. There was no amount of ego, will or clock-time that could serve me in this process, any more than we can hasten a fruit to ripen or rush a flower to bloom. It seems that healing invariably takes more time than anyone imagines, and so I am being reshaped by patience, watching and listening.

Like water nourishing a landscape, if I slow down, I can go deeper. This shift in my inner pacing, staying attuned to my body's needs, is helping me come home to my self.

Another of the gifts of this underworld journey is
discovering that healing my vision requires rest, and that rest is
more than the absence of activity. In a similar way that darkness
involves far more than only the absence of light, I had to learn how
to surrender and commit myself — fully and consciously — to the
benefits and gifts of resting.

As the famous mystic, theologian and Trappist monk Thomas
Merton wrote in *Conjectures of a Guilty Bystander*: "The rush and
pressure of modern life are a form, perhaps the most common
form, of innate violence. To allow oneself to be carried away by
a multitude of conflicting concerns, to surrender to too many
demands, to commit oneself to too many projects, to want to help
everyone in everything is to succumb to violence. More than that,
it is cooperation with violence. The frenzy of the activist neutralizes
his work for peace. It destroys her own inner capacity for peace. It
destroys the fruitfulness of our own work, because it kills the root of
inner wisdom which makes work fruitful."

I've learned that rest comes in many flavors and textures.
For repair and for inviting vision, it likes solitude and stillness, and
sometimes communing with an animal, a tree or a cup of tea. It savors
emptiness, stillness, and the invitation to welcome whatever comes.
There are no instructions for rest's fulfillment; I could learn its needs
only by tracking, observing and listening inwardly.

May we practice surrendering to Mother Life's own rhythms
and pacing for healing ourselves and our cultures. May we practice
humbly listening, sensing and watching for what our bodies and the
Earth's know, want and need. May we practice actively seeing each other
with our inner eyes, and in so doing invite each other toward fullness,
fruition and flourishing.

May we give ourselves wholeheartedly to loving, tending and celebrating *all* of our Earth relatives, so that our children's children might still know whales, elephants, bears, giraffes, tigers, lions, orangutans, bonobos, and old-growth forests, pristine grasslands, clean flowing rivers, and bountiful, life-enhancing oceans.

Amen, Awomen, Aho.

FROM MOURNING INTO DAYBREAK

How will we ever see daybreak without mourning?

If we don't feel what hurts, surrender to its demands,
  speak the wound,
how can we really begin to heal?

When my father died,
I felt the rock I stood on
  suddenly gone, my identity lost, in free fall.

A friend warned it might take a year for me to heal.
It was longer, and
I was grateful for the crystalline time.

Long, elastic months of feeling transparent,
  of squinting at the striking brightness of colors, lines and light,
of oscillating between emptiness and attunement,
the tenderness of tears always a breath away.

I was appalled to discover our illiteracy toward death,
and envied a Japanese tradition I'd heard about,

of wearing a black armband for a year following the loss of a
    loved one,
    so that everyone knows not to treat you in the usual way.

Walking in the shimmering New Mexico light,
    a huge crow swoops to meet me.
His large beak stuttering open,
    he croaks his hello, frog-like,
        focused on me, inciting a conversation.

When I respond, he flies closer, perches to stare at me,
    beady black eyes glow against shiny indigo feathers.

He caws in clusters of three,
his wings inflating with each inhale,
Cccaaaawwww, cccaaawww, ccccaaawwww.

My responding calls intrigue him, and we converse,
    an arc of connection cutting through
the apple-crisp autumn air.

He pauses, turning his head to an improbable angle
    to suck water through his long thin beak
        from the shallow pool puddled in the cement birdbath.

I wonder if he is a bird of sorrow,
    or a creature of connection,
and then I know he is both.

I learned this duality exists from my father,
    a man whose lion heart was far too big
for the losses his love suffered in its youth.

But his affection was a tender bath of papa-love,
    the sun I basked in when I was small,
arms I could count on.

Isn't it strange,
    how unspeakably beautiful life becomes
when death draws near?

It hovers close now, all the time,
    with extinctions everywhere,
1,800 species disappearing every day —
    my mind reels at it, staggering.

The tundra melting,
    trees tilting drunkenly as they lose their ground,
entire cultures losing their lifeways,
    the terrain too erratic for hunting anymore.

Who mourns these losses?

How can we not go mad with grief?

Afraid I'll start wailing, I rock inwardly, and don't stop.
Yearning to speak out, I feel fearful.
The voices within me are at once so young, agitated,

and also ancient, sitting stone-still and calm.

They know the words that must be spoken, but
    giving them voice raises quaking fear within me.
I ask that the elder hold the young one,
    to lend her stillness, offer her strength.

How will we grieve
for the vividly colored corals bleached white,
    for the animals brutally hunted,
        for all those whose habitats have been logged
    to make mail-order catalogs, phonebooks,
        toilet paper and newspapers?

The crone wants to shake us all awake, screeching
Don't you get it?
This is no time for small talk.
This is a time for mythmaking.
This is a time for epic poetry.
This is a time to tell the tales
    that will become our compass
        for the days ahead.

A time to remember the grace
    and celebrate the magic
        that infuses and informs this world.

We live on the only planet we know of
    where the sun and moon appear the same size,

the only planet where an eclipse is possible.

Doesn't that seem like instructions to you?

To awaken from this self-induced slumber,
    to emerge from this contracted isolation,
we've got to drink down the darkness
    and dive to our deepest fathoms,
peel off our fancy garments
    of presumed protection
to land at the bottom, naked, cold and bruised,
    with nowhere to go but up.

Time to shed the venom that got us here,
    the red rage of blame and shame,
and choose instead to embrace the outrage that
       rises, pure and clean, up through our feet,
that draws us to our full height,
    knowing what must be done,
sparking us to stand up for what we love.

How else can we begin the healing?

Indra's web is dangling
    and can't be repaired with Band-Aids.
Only our tears can begin to mend its tattered strands,
    tears and giving ourselves to keening, pining, grieving
mourning how much is dying,
    mourning so that the light can return.

The revolution must have dancing, women know this.

The music will light our hearts on fire,
The stories will bathe our dreams in honey
    and fill our bellies with stars.
The interlacing of our souls enlarging our humanity,
    our rhythms will merge with the heartbeat of the Earth.

What breaks the mourning open for me?
It shines through my connections, my friends, my kin
    some who are human, and some who are not.

I soar in the sea, glide stealthily among sea turtles and
    swoop over snowpack like an eagle.

I am lifted by the courageous uprisings
    of women and girls,
and of the emerging voice of the feminine within us all.

And I am strengthened
    by my kinship with the land,
with the high desert hills of New Mexico.

At dusk, I wander down the arroyo by our house.
Further up the same canyon,
    flanked by crisscrossing dogs chasing scents,
        a crow swoops low over my left shoulder, cawing.

At the bottom I stop, standing still on a sandy spit
    savoring the dry, clean air of the ponderosa forest.
Glancing down, a perfect white shell catches my eye,
    spiraling pristinely,
        speaking to me in sacred whispers of a life long before
my own.

As my friend Akaya Windwood reminds me,
    the world shifts every time a woman speaks her truth.

May it be so.

REINVENTING LEADERSHIP

Reclaiming the Feminine

Interview with Lauren Schiller, Host of "Inflection Point" a podcast about how women rise up.

The following is edited excerpts of a longer interview from May, 2017.

Lauren Schiller: *As you made your way through your career and discovered what your skills and talents were, did you think of yourself as a leader? Did you have a certain style that you were trying to create or emulate?*

Nina Simons: I don't think I ever thought of myself as a leader. Now that I can reflect back on it I think that in some ways my tendency to be extroverted and my love of connecting with people was a tremendous skill and asset for me, and it encouraged a kind of natural leadership in me. I followed what I did well, and that meant building teams of people and helping groups orient toward a common vision and a common goal.

With Seeds of Change I remember discovering that I had a knack for business although I had never been to business school. Learning that I was good at managing budgets and writing business plans was a total surprise to me, and what I realized was that as long as I was really honest about saying what I didn't know and that the people who I was working with were OK with that, then I could stumble my way along and learn as I went. Those natural pragmatic talents that I had around business and people served me well, and I didn't think much about it until my late thirties, when I was acknowledged by a magazine, *The Utne Reader*, for being an up-and-coming leader. And I remember being simultaneously honored and horrified. I felt so uncomfortable about it.

I wasn't even sure why I was so uncomfortable. I realized afterwards I felt like it painted a target on my chest and it felt egotistical to me in a way that made me squirm. It felt like a label that I had never aspired to. And yet I knew from my work with Bioneers that what the world needed was for us all to become leaders.

I wondered whether, if I had this reaction to being called a leader, then maybe other people do too. The more women I talked to, the more I learned that most of us have a really negative reaction to calling ourselves leaders. As I began to unpack that, I realized that I had all kinds of belief systems, images and ideas (that I had never consciously adopted, but that were in me nonetheless), about what leadership was and what it looked like. And I didn't want to be any of those things.

LS: It's so interesting — especially nowadays when everyone is trying to get 15 minutes of fame through a personal brand on social media. People are putting as many photos of themselves and selfies out there as they possibly can. I mean, talk about putting a target on your chest, and then being featured in a magazine as an up-and-coming leader under 40. I would imagine many people probably aspire to that as a career goal, right? And yet your reaction to it was so negative.

NS: I think part of that was because I grew up with a model in my head that said service to others is good and selfishness is not. As a result, my sense of identity was really built around being of service to the greater good. And also, I'd had the gift of producing Bioneers for many years and witnessing and meeting hundreds of leaders from all backgrounds and walks of life. I certainly didn't want to be a leader if that meant being aggressive and dominating, charismatic, hierarchical and putting other people down. Those were my previous associations with leadership, but many of the figures who spoke at Bioneers weren't like that, so I thought, 'Well, who are the leaders who really inspire me? If I can get clear about that and understand what they are doing, I can begin to see models I can emulate and perhaps grow into.'

What I found when I looked for themes and patterns was that the leaders I respected and admired most were humble. They were leading change because of something that they really loved and felt passionate about, and most often they didn't have formal training to do it. No one gave them a degree or a job or a crown, but they served something they really believed in. Through that devotion and focus and passion, they attracted other people to get involved, and in many cases they led collaboratively. They led by raising up other leaders. They were not really interested in being in the spotlight. Their goal — contrary to the current Instagram and Facebook world — was to save a redwood forest or sea turtles and the ocean or to create peace in the world. And if I was going to be leader, that was the kind of leader I aspired to be.

As a result of that inquiry, I co-edited with Anneke Campbell an anthology book called *Moonrise: The Power of Women Leading from the Heart*, which is an homage to my mentors.

LS: And when you were exploring all these leaders, were these all women, or did you start with both men and women?

NS: I have to admit to having had a certain bias for women at that point. I had had an epiphany moment earlier in my life when I was turned on to a film called *The Burning Times* that tells the story of the 300-year period in European history where millions of women were systematically persecuted and tortured, and many were burned at the stake for the supposed crime of being witches.

The film changed my worldview because for the first time I saw that all of the problems that I had learned about from Bioneers could be seen as a function of the imbalance between the masculine and the feminine in our culture.

Investigating further, I learned that women had owned more wealth in Europe than men before that period, but not after. That centuries-long war that the church sustained against women created a huge transfer of resources from women to men. Also, a number of social systems and institutions that had largely been under the purview of women (folk healers, herbalists, midwives, etc.) were radically upended and reinvented by men. By the end of the Burning Times only men could practice medicine, for example.

Of course these events occurred in Europe, but this patriarchal legacy has affected women everywhere. For instance, in Central and South America, and throughout Africa, colonialism brought systematic persecution of women folk healers as well.

With the emergence of Christianity, European culture shifted away from a largely earth-based, polytheistic culture to a patriarchy where religion was practiced in a church and led by a priest who intermediated between people and the divine. From what had been a direct, widely shared, community-wide connection with nature and the sacred, most forms of spiritual practice became mediated by male authority figures, and women lost much of their previous authority and autonomy. The period of the "burning times" was the final brutal, violent nail in the coffin of that process.

It's a huge story and one that I believe explains a lot. I did have a bias toward women when I began seeking models of new leadership styles. I saw that embedded gender bias or lopsidedness as being equally true in men as it is in women. In my view, regardless of our gender, we all have that internal bias that needs to be healed and rebalanced, if we are to live healthy and fully effective lives.

That said, I found that there were some wonderful men who were also personifying leading from the heart, and it became important to me to include them in the book. My publisher was very uncertain and said: "Are you sure? This is a women's book. Why are we putting men in it?" I said: "Because this is a model of leadership that anyone can practice, so we must lift these men up as models for others to see."

LS: That just solidifies the idea that none of us is one thing or the other, that we can carry both "gendered" traits with us, and we don't always have to behave in the future the way we've behaved in the past.

NS: Well that's for sure. One of the gifts of being human is our capacity for change. What I am advocating is what I would call "blended" or "full-spectrum" leadership, in that I want to be able to draw from a full spectrum of all my human capacities, which of course includes everything within our humanity, from yin to yang. It includes a full array of ways of being. Thankfully, I see younger generations as being already much more fluid in that spectrum than people my age, but it's clear to me that for us to meet this moment of life on earth that's asking so much from us in leadership, we need all of ourselves present, and

that means addressing the shadow of women's leadership, which I think
is part of that root story.

*LS: Let me ask you this: What would you say that the things people value
in a leader are, and what percentage of them would you say are considered
masculine traits?*

NS: I think that the traits people valued in leaders of yesteryear
were rationality, decisiveness, aggression, and strength, as well as
endurance, stoicism and perseverance. Not that any of those things are
bad — they're all great. There's a great book called *The Athena Doctrine*
which describes how of the huge data pool of people that they polled
in 13 nations around the world, 67 percent said the world would be a
better place if more people led like women. What they are referring to
is that the leaders that are being prized now are being appreciated for
their capacity to listen, their open-mindedness, for their ability to stay
calm in stressful and challenging situations, for their emotional and
relational intelligence, and for their ability to evaluate context and the
big picture and consider complex dynamics.

    I think that what *The Athena Doctrine* is pointing to is that
there's evidence from all sectors that the more women there are in
leadership in corporations and on boards, the better the bottom lines
of those enterprises are and the more ethical their governance. In
governance and diplomacy, the more women are involved, the more
peaceful things tend to be. The evidence is consistent and pretty
astounding, coming from every sector and direction. It's important to
note that this is not about putting down men. It's about saying we're
all in a giant shift in relation to those gendered definitions that we've
all absorbed without questioning them previously.

One of my favorite metaphors comes from some Indigenous groups who say that the bird of humanity has been trying to fly with only one wing for far too long and needs now to be balanced for all of us to survive and thrive.

LS: That's just such a great visual. I can see the bird flying in circles but not getting anywhere. And I would say that pretty much sums up the state of affairs at this particular moment.

NS: Although my other favorite metaphor is that we're living through a time when the dying dinosaur of the patriarchy is flailing its tail and doing as much damage as it knows how to do on its way out, and it's scary and unsettling and is asking a lot of all of us.

LS: It's so true. And one of the ways that it's manifesting itself — at least from what I've observed and what I've heard — is that women who try and lead "like men" are experiencing a backlash against that, they're actually not rewarded for working in that way. And that's now a bind, like "What am I supposed to do it if that's the way we're supposed to lead, but I'm going to get penalized for being like a man?" If we can start to embrace some of these other ways of approaching leadership and having that be valued it certainly seems like a step in the right direction.

NS: I completely agree. It takes a lot of personal courage to do that, because it's risky. And the truth is there's a lot of implicit bias in all of us. I had an interesting experience recently: a young woman who had taken one of our women's leadership trainings and who is a consultant in the Bay Area contacted me about a company that she was consulting to and she said "They've asked me to give them a proposal to shift so that in five years they're going to be known as one of the best places for women to work. Will you help me?" And I said "Yes, but do they have any idea what they're taking on?" The more we talked, what became apparent was that it's not just about adopting women-friendly and family-friendly policies, although those are really important. What about educating the men? I mean you really have to shift the whole system to truly address gender bias, and that's deep work that requires time and commitment.

LS: Will there ever be an end to that? I mean what will it take for that shift to happen, so that we're no longer fighting the system but we've created a system in which both the masculine and feminine are valued?

NS: I think we'll get there, but I'm optimistic by nature. There's evidence of it when I look at couples in their 20s and 30s raising children right now. There's an awful lot more sharing of housework and parenting. I see how beautifully their parents just pass the ball, sharing the workload, and there's no expectation about what's mom's role and what's dad's role. They're just co-parenting. So, I think there's a lot of evidence of change. I think it's a generational shift that we're experiencing. I also think this is related to how we heal from systems of privilege and bias because white privilege and racial bias obviously intersect with gender biases.

Just being a white woman in this country confers privilege, and that privilege creates blinders. It took me a long time to understand that I had privilege compared to women of color and to move beyond guilt or shame about it, so that I could start to try to make a difference and transform that biased system at its roots.

It's very hard to get out of patterns that seem so pervasive, entrenched and "normal" in our culture. Women all know the experience of being in a mostly-male meeting and initiating an idea or suggestion and having it fall on deaf ears, and then the guy next to you says the same thing with slightly different language and everybody jumps on it. Every woman around nods her head when someone complains about that because it's something we've all experienced countless times. Men, however, however don't notice it when it happens, and it's not anyone's fault as an individual. The challenge is to become aware of the blinders that privilege creates for us.

LS: Tell me about some of the work you've been doing with women's leadership training.

NS: For the last 12 years, we have been developing a program that we called Cultivating Women's Leadership within Bioneers. It's a six-day immersion experience that we invite women to apply for and then select each cohort of 20 women very carefully. We've selected women using a number of criteria. One criterion, for example, was how passionate they are about making change in the world because those are the women we most want to work with. Another is what evidence we can find of this woman being able to influence change in her community. Yet another criterion (which is perhaps the most interesting) is that we've selected each group to optimize for diversity in every way. What that means is that each cohort typically has women ranging in age from their 20s to their 70s or 80s. We've intentionally selected for the most diverse group, across ethnic diversity and class, and across sexual orientation and issue area, sector or discipline.

So we get a group of women who in normal life in our country would never get to encounter each other in a deep way and give them six days to do a lot of deep work both on an individual level and with each other. By the end of the six days, what's been remarkable is that very often those women have bonded really deeply with each other, and they've formed connections that are lasting years later, which is part of our intention. So that's been a journey, and we always knew that it was important to us to have a lot of age and racial diversity in the room.

In the early days of the program, it was harder to attract the mix we wished for, partly because at that time I was doing most of the facilitating with my co-founder Toby Herzlich, who is another white woman. When women of color saw our fliers and saw the program being led by two white women, they likely figured it wasn't for them.

Then I read a book by Linda Tarr Whelan called *Women Lead the Way*. What I learned was that there is social science research that shows that for any members of a minority to fully show up in a group, they need to comprise at least 30 percent of the room. Until they're at 30 percent, they just don't feel flanked enough to take the risks to relax, be outspoken, and really be themselves.

I reflected on that in relation to the percentage of women in our U.S. House and Senate, which is not even remotely close, still well under 20 percent. We decided that from that point forward we would always have a minimum of 30 percent women of color in our groups, and we invited facilitators who are women of color to join us, so that there was always a third facilitator so that one third of us in facilitation was a woman of color. As soon as we did that, we started getting 35 to 40 percent women of color in our trainings. And that's been an incredible teaching for me and really interesting in terms of all the things we're talking about from the boardroom to classrooms to, in this case, learning environments and gathering groups together well.

LS: *Could we apply that 30 percent rule to other situations? You just brought up the House and Senate.*

NS: Yes, I believe so. In fact, our political and economic institutions don't remotely reflect the demographics of our nation, not only in gender but in color and class and in just about every other way. So, yes, reaching at least 30 percent would make a big difference. There's evidence and data that proves it, and quite a few countries are far ahead of us. Some Scandinavian political parties have actual quotas in the 40 to 50 percent range for women candidates, and Sweden's parliament was, last time I checked, around 45 percent women.

There's another piece to this too. Through the work I've been doing, I've come to believe that mothering is one of the greatest acts of leadership that any woman can do in her life. And we're all trying to recover from a culture that has so systematically devalued mothering and degraded it. Often, I find that mothers who are also leaders who do this work with us are so grateful to have motherhood appreciated as the act of leadership that it is. I'm in awe of mothers, as a woman who is childless by choice. In many ways, I get to mother a lot of women, but in other ways I just look at what women who are mothers do, many of them also juggling leadership roles in the world, and I am just gobsmacked. It's amazing.

LS: *How exciting to imagine the generation of kids that are growing up now with really strong models of fathers who can cook and love them and read to them and snuggle with them and who don't chew them out for crying or feeling. It's exciting...As we try and imagine our future, putting a higher value on motherhood is a good thing for many reasons. I think not many people would argue with that, but right now, according to very* *credible research, if you are a woman and you have a child, your lifetime income is almost certain to be 20 to 30 percent less than a man of same age in the same position.*

NS: There was a *New York Times* article recently about Janet Yellen (the former chair of the Federal Reserve Bank) speaking at Brown University. She said that the best thing we could do to grow the economy and develop jobs is to adopt the family-friendly maternity practices and reproductive rights practices that nearly all of Europe has adopted, because it would allow us to support so many more women to be in the workplace. So, in terms of job creation and our nation's economic bottom line, we absolutely need more family-friendly policies and practices.

LS: *I'd love to talk more about how you ultimately embraced your role as a leader after* The Utne Reader *honored you, why you felt so conflicted about it, and how you came to terms with yourself?*

NS: I had this big turning point moment 20 years ago when I turned 40. I made myself several promises, and one was that I would seek to understand and unpack this leadership conundrum that I'd gotten into. Another was that I decided that I needed to learn to live more from my feminine side, to better balance myself inwardly. All my friends said, "Are you kidding, you're so feminine." I said, "Well it may look that way to you, but on the inside, I can tell you the way I've navigated my adult life has been through what I have experienced as my more masculine qualities."

I had relied heavily on my intellect, my capacity for strategic thinking and my strong body to power through situations and to persevere at all costs. Many parts of me felt underutilized and under-acknowledged, so I began exploring what they were, and every cell in my body said "yes." When I started attending to those underused parts of me, something deep inside me was feeling affirmed. I began to pay more attention to my dreams and my intuition. Basically, I'd been ignoring my body's wisdom. Part of the inheritance of a biased culture has been that we value the intellect over all of our other ways of knowing.

I went through a conscious process of trying to turn up the volume on all of my other ways of knowing and practice valuing them. Part of how I did that was through gathering and facilitating groups of women. The first time I gathered women was in 2002. I convened women leaders for a gathering called Unreasonable Women for the Earth. I invited 35 accomplished and very diverse women, letting my intuition guide me. I had no idea what I was doing. I sensed into it and made it all up as I went along. We spent four or five days together in a very beautiful place. Among other outcomes, the very dynamic direct action group, CODEPINK: Women for Peace, emerged from some of the women present during that retreat. I learned that the name you organize under deeply affects the outcome.

LS: So, for you what came out of it in terms of how you approached the work that you had set out to do?

NS: As I reclaimed all these parts of myself, I saw how women who could embrace and stand with their own vulnerability and their own intuition and their own body wisdom and their dreams and playfulness and humor could mobilize to act. I saw how powerful that could be. Since I aspired to it, I think I cultivated myself to become more and more like that. In many ways, the Cultivating Women's Leadership retreats of the last 12 years have cultivated me and my colleagues as well as all the women who have been through it. When I started doing those retreats, I had a lot of ideas about what women should do and what kind of leadership was needed. I very quickly disabused myself of those ideas as I realized that women were showing up in more shapes and forms, styles and assignments than I could ever have imagined.

I saw that my job, my purpose, became not to tell anyone what they should do (because it's hard enough for me to know what I should do) but rather to create the conditions for them to discover for themselves how their best expression in the world could manifest (or *womanifest* as we like to say it).

That's given me a lot of hope because I've realized that this great uprising, which we're all part of and which is so urgently needed to save humanity from ourselves, will include many more facets and modalities than I can even dream of. I long ago stopped saying "to save the Earth" because the Earth will survive — it may take her two or three million years to get over us — but she'll survive. It's really we who are in danger here, and so leadership is needed, I believe, in as many forms now as there are humans on the planet There is leadership that we need to learn from all the other-than-human life in the biosphere as well, from the trees and the fungi and the insects and animals and creatures of all kinds.

LS: Would you say that leading from the feminine and leading from the heart are interchangeable expressions or would you define them slightly differently?

NS: I think we're in a time where language can be a trap. Leading from the heart is much more accessible to most people. However, for me, it's not the same because leading from the feminine is bigger than leading from the heart. It includes leading from your connection to the divine or sacred as well and also from intuition and your body's senses and awareness. I think they're all intelligences that have been chronically undervalued. For me, leading from the feminine includes all those realms, and not just the heart.

LS: It's so refreshing. I just feel like we're living in this world that is being led by fear and that all of the decisions being made at the governmental, corporate and even sometimes family levels are based on fear. What you're talking about feels like the complete opposite.

NS: Yes, we are living through a time when pretty much anyone alive and paying attention is dealing with some post-traumatic stress. Among young people growing up with climate instability, increasing economic inequality, persistent racial injustice, gun violence, etc., chronic stress is rampant.

What I am interested in is how to develop the capacity for resilience in ourselves as leaders, and some of that means going against the tide. With things speeding up so much, and so much media and information coming at us all the time, it's so important to slow down and go inside for guidance to inform our actions.

There's a very interesting correlation to all this stuff about the feminine that I love and remind myself about often. Carl Jung suggested that the feminine is our interiority and the masculine represents our exterior. When you think about all that fear-based, panic-driven emotion, it's very reactive and externally focused. It's about pursuing some imagined safety or security that probably isn't very real.

The only real security lies inwardly and in our relationships, through a web of connection to the people we love and who love us and also to the places and creatures we love and whatever it is we love; that's the only real security. We all know that the economy will shed millions of jobs due to technological change and other factors, so the notion that you're going to have a straight up career and then retire with a gold watch is so over. It's not happening anymore.

We need to shift our understanding of what security really means. For me what's also exciting about the path that keeps revealing itself to me is that it involves inviting people into a life of meaning. There's an awful lot of distraction out there. It's part of the work we do in these women's leadership retreats. We do something we call a purpose marathon; it's a very long afternoon during which we engage in a lot of repeated questioning. It's sort of like peeling an onion; you go deeper and deeper inside yourself to notice what really lights you up. What do you really love dearly? What has been a really resonant or important thing for you all your life? What breaks your heart?

I know that when I read stories about whales dying of stomach cancer because of all the plastic inside them, it breaks my heart. When I learn about the rate of extinctions and that a number of large mammal species could go extinct in the coming decades, it really hurts. I don't know or care why that is. I care that it motivates me and that it's a way to help me identify my deepest passion. As I see it, the work of this time is for each of us to find what we're most exactly called to do and then invest ourselves fully there.

I used to be very impatient about finding my path. I asked someone I viewed as a guide how I might become clearer about it. She suggested that I invest in my longing. She said, "your longing lives in a chamber behind your heart, and if you invest your attention there, it will attract to you the path that your soul is here to walk." And I didn't know if I believed in it or not, but I tried it, and I think it works!

LS: Maybe because instead of fighting to figure out what you want, you're embracing figuring out what you want.

NS: Partly yes, but also instead of trying to figure out what I wanted with my head, I invested in my heart's yearning, and it guided me. Einstein said something like: "…we should take care not to make the intellect our god; it has, of course, powerful muscles, but no personality. It cannot lead, it can only serve; and it is not fastidious in its choice of a leader."

LS: What's the best advice that you've ever been given about how to slow down?

NS: A couple of things come to mind. One piece of advice was also about identifying one's purpose, but it's related to how to slow down and how to listen inwardly. I had a wise woman tell me to "pay exquisite attention inwardly to what makes your flame grow brighter." She said you have to be very still and pay a lot of attention because sometimes that flame just perks up only for an instant. If you're not paying exquisite attention, you'll miss it. That was great guidance, and it's necessary to slow down to practice it.

The other thing: I'm teaching a workshop on regenerative leadership with a woman who is a wonderful relational mindfulness teacher named Deborah Eden Tull, who lived in a Zen monastery for seven years. I think what she has done is to feminize Buddhist practice, meditation and Zen by inventing this idea and practice of relational mindfulness, and she's just written a book by that title. She teaches that meditation is the subtlest form of self-love. I can't profess to say that I'm a great meditator because I'm not, but there is a quality of really deep listening inwardly to all the parts of yourself that feels to me like a great way to slow down. The other way that I practice a lot is by being truly present and attentive in nature. I always find that when I'm depressed, stressed, freaked out or confused, being alone in nature is my solace.

LS: *Thank you so much, Nina.*

PART II

Women's Leadership

THE CHALLENGES, THE PATHWAYS
AND THE PROMISE

AT THE FRONT LINES

The Global War on Women

A few years ago, I hosted a panel at the UN Commission on the Status of Women focused on Women, Health and Extractive Industries. I already knew that women were frequently on the frontlines, but I had not realized the systematized ways in which corporations globally have targeted women in their efforts to plunder the Earth. I had not fully understood the cascading detriments to their communities nor the staggering worldwide extent of the deployment of this gendered tactic.

Whether mining for coal, gems or metal ores, drilling or fracking for oil, multinationals move into often rural communities, frequently Indigenous communities, and the first thing they do is to establish "man camps" for all the workers they bring in. The women in these often-remote regions are the first to be impacted, as rape, sex trafficking, prostitution and domestic abuse reach epidemic levels. And the local men aren't spared either, as they experience sharp rises in alcoholism, drug abuse, poverty and joblessness. This not only decimates families as it demolishes landscapes, it destroys entire traditional lifeways, cultures and languages.

At that UN event, women from many nations rose and spoke. Listening, as I heard these very different people from all over the planet all tell similar stories and speak of their anguish at the destruction of their communities, my stomach recoiled in anger. I recognized at that event how systemic, entrenched and brutal the global war on women really is.

When I got still enough to listen to my heart, however, I was enlivened by their courage, and inspired by the outrage in their voices. I remembered that anger is our body's way of telling us a boundary has been trespassed. I felt in a deeper way how interconnected their lives, mine and ours really are.

Indigenous communities worldwide have long been especially hard hit by corporations and governments run amok, sustaining intergenerational histories of relocations, broken treaties, forced sterilization, systemic racism, and land theft. Many of them have been in recent decades showing the world that they are incredibly resilient, organizing and fighting back, which is extraordinary after 500 years of brutal oppression, expropriation and focused attempts to annihilate their cultures, knowledge systems and ecosystems.

When my heart takes this in, integrating what Ta-Nehisi Coates calls the "bloody heirloom" of systemic racial injustice that pervades the history of this country, I am stunned by the rot in the foundations of this nation, by the profound and largely still invisible and unacknowledged legacy of theft, deceit and violence that the U.S. was built upon.

A woman leader of huge heart and spirit I know, a single mother of three, told me of leaving her home in Oakland one morning. As she left for work, there was yellow police tape across her neighbor's door — a woman she knew had been shot while trying to protect her kids. Arriving to her workplace at Bayview Hunter's Point, where she worked to save the lives of young brown and black girls, she found the same tape there. Many of our fellow citizens are living in war zones, right here at home. Extreme poverty, environmental degradation and violence don't just exist in other, distant lands.

At one of our Cultivating Women's Leadership intensives, a majority of the women there had been raped or abused at least once. I wondered about the effects of so much violation, but as our days unfolded, I was struck by their strength, stunned by their resilience and humbled by their commitments, their visions and resolve. Their dignity, their pride in their own recovery and their purposeful ways of transforming society were so solid, so strong, and so creative that I was awed and inspired by their character. Violence against women is a global pandemic of immense proportions, and relatively few among us recognize how prevalent and systemic it really is.

Although in 1993 the UN General Assembly declared a framework for ending global violence against women, over twenty years later, little has improved. Try wrapping your mind around these statistics, from the United Nations and the World Health Organization:

- Around the world, at least 35 percent of women have been beaten, raped or otherwise physically abused in their lifetimes.

- Intimate partners commit between 40 and 70 percent of the homicides of women worldwide.

- Women perform two thirds of the world's work, while earning 10 percent of global income and owning only 1 percent of global financial assets.

- Of the billion or so poorest people on earth living in poverty, 70 percent are women.

- An estimated two hundred million women and girls alive today in thirty nations around the globe are victims of female genital mutilation.

- No one knows the exact numbers, but, globally, up to four million women and girls are estimated to be trafficked annually, with an estimated one million children, mostly girls, entering the sex trade each year.

And in *this* country:

- At least one in six women is a victim of domestic or sexual assault.

- Among Indigenous people, that number is closer to four of every five.

- Every fifteen seconds a woman is battered, usually by her intimate partner, and it's suspected that only about half the incidents are reported.

- Among girls between the ages of twelve and sixteen, 83 percent report having experienced some form of sexual harassment in school.

And far too often insidious, self-limiting, culturally reinforced beliefs and stories keep women from leaving abusive relationships.

The promise of a women-led revolution will not happen if we continue to sabotage ourselves and view ourselves in competition with our sisters. Many of us have been conditioned to give away our power, ending our sentences with question marks, or apologizing when we don't really mean to. We do these things to please others or to avoid conflict. We agree to things we don't really want and have a hard time asking for what we need. We deflect compliments and are typically far more comfortable giving than receiving.

It's an arduous and lengthy journey building the conscious muscle of acceptance, self-respect and self-love through self-awareness so that we can resist those patterns, and cultivate new ones, but it is doable, and the payoff is larger and more enduring, I've found, than any other task you might imagine. It's not really our power we're reclaiming, anyway; it's actually the power of mother life coming through us. It's the power of spirit, the power of ancestors. It's the power of something far greater than any of us.

Meeting women from Serbia in Taos, New Mexico, I saw light shining from their eyes. Even as I learned about the horrors they had experienced, I could feel the power of their playful and buoyant hearts. I learned their ancient Kolo dance, a restorative ritual that's been practiced by women since Mesolithic times. The women, encircled tightly, clasp hands over the fronts and backs of each other's wombs and then, very close together, dance for hours. Their ways of dancing and singing together have contributed to helping heal thousands who've been raped and traumatized in their wars.

When women are truly aligned by authenticity and agree to stand for and with each other, to have each other's backs and become practice partners, magic becomes possible. In some Mexican communities, they may become comadres, and enter a lifelong pact, which includes promising to care for each other's children if either of them cannot. Despite the insidious and deeply encoded beliefs that assign women to interiority, to the home and child-raising and away from the risk-taking challenges of leadership, many of us are ready to pull the ripcord that may unleash us all and and give us the confidence that exactly who and what we already are — especially when we come together — is enough to accomplish our goals.

I've learned that motherhood is among the greatest and most courageous learning curves in life that anyone has ever attempted (whoever imagines that parenting isn't leadership clearly hasn't tried it!).

In Cultivating Women's Leadership intensives over the years, among women leaders selected for their diversity in all ways — across age, race, orientation, faith and discipline — once the women see each other in all their dimensional beauty and power, hear each other's visions for changing the world, and witness the depth of caring, and the skillfulness that each brings to her work, the sisterhood they experience emboldens each one to step out and shine more fully.

Intergenerationally, the friendships that have formed between women in their eighties and others in their twenties agreeing to be mutual mentors, with reciprocity and respect, have ignited my heart with tender appreciation, hope and delight. Witnessing varying versions of this phenomenon over the past many years has strengthened my vision, my appreciation and my investment in connecting bold and committed women across the differences that far too often divide us.

As Shannon Thunderbird, a Coast Tsimshian elder, notes: "We are Mother Earth's heartbeat, the life-givers; it is our responsibility to bring peace, harmony and balance back to the world." Her words reinforce what life's shown me repeatedly — that women have extraordinary capacities when they are in authentic and deep alignment. Together we can heal, transform and radically grow each other's capacity to lead our communities and our cultures toward a world that is healthy, loving, peaceful and regenerative.

We are being called upon to connect across our divides, to come together in solidarity to defend and protect the sanctity of all life, knowing that we will find the greatest creative opportunities and options in the places where edges meet, to constellate together a web of co-creativity and mutuality on behalf of mother Earth and the entire web of life. All around us, the old structures of dominance are both overreaching and crumbling, and though at times the forces we're up against may seem impossible to overcome, I believe that women's amazing capacity to heal, grow and strengthen each other is likely the single greatest underutilized resource we have, as a species, for transforming our world.

GRASSROOTS WOMEN

Restoring Relations Around the World

O ne of the most promising phenomena in recent years has been the emergence around the world of grassroots women-led movements that are creating solutions to social and environmental problems by reconnecting relationships — not only between people, but also between people and the land, creating cascading positive effects, restoring economic stability, peace and ecological health.

These women leaders are making visible previously invisible connections among seemingly disparate issues or constituencies, creating connective tissue to align people in common cause. They are creating conditions for solidarity in ways that sometimes involve unusual alliances of strange bedfellows. Coming out of a culture that tends to separate and divide us, I believe this is one of the most crucial strategies we need to adopt in this pivotal time.

A recent, striking example of that is the remarkable mobilization (with only ten weeks for planning!) of coordinated marches to resist the misogynist, xenophobic and racist attitudes and actions of incoming President Donald Trump. Planned rapidly by four grassroots women organizers of very diverse backgrounds and ethnicities (one of whom had a baby during the planning phase), and then organized in a decentralized fashion in over 600 cities throughout the U.S. and the world, the Women's March of January 20, 2017 broke records for the largest turnouts of demonstrators in U.S. history. Globally, another 60 marches occurred around the world.

Many have estimated the turnout as collectively in the several millions, sending a clear message to the president on his first day in office. Referring to it as the "Inclusion Revolution," the march, while predominantly female, included men, a spectrum of LGBTQ people, immigrant families, black and Latina and Indigenous speakers and performers, and many mothers and daughters, and the rallying cries were for solidarity, bold love, standing together and continuing to resist. Stunningly, there was no violence and there were no arrests.

Although the weeks and months that followed revealed fissures in the movement — examples abounded of groups that had felt snubbed or disrespected, revealing just how much social healing and repair is yet to be done — the embodiment of solidarity across divides that the events globally represented was profoundly historically significant and provided a beacon of hope in dark times.

Many other current examples of women's leadership also exemplify approaches to problems that the agrarian philosopher, poet and activist Wendell Berry characterized as "solving for pattern." There are, he notes, many well-meaning solutions that create new problems or make the existing ones worse. Creating a dam across a river to build a reservoir, for example, might help regulate water flows and help irrigate crops and generate power, but dams often displace whole communities and can drastically degrade large ecosystems and all the species living in them. An ideal, elegant solution looks at a problem in relationship to the larger patterns within which it is embedded. This kind of solution, Berry asserts, solves more than the problem it is meant to address. It has a positive influence on a whole web of relationships, increasing the vitality of an entire system. It can result in what he calls "cascading benefits," generating positive outcomes affecting many dimensions of a landscape or a community.

Around the world women are cooking up systemic solutions to problems that are based on respect for the people, land and cultures involved, and often they are forging coalitions and catalyzing collaboration among thousands of people to effect change. In the Niger Delta a few years ago, for example, hundreds of women blocked the gates of Chevron/Texaco in protests demanding that the company provide jobs, schools and hospitals, as well as clean up the toxic chemicals in their water. Within 36 hours of beginning this action, as word spread throughout the countryside, they were spontaneously joined by thousands more women in their nonviolent occupation. A turning point was reached in the negotiations when the women threatened to take off their clothes — a powerful traditional shaming gesture — to humiliate the company.

These peaceful, all-woman protests were a major departure from past attempts at pressuring oil multinationals to change, which have frequently involved armed men using kidnapping and sabotage to get the corporations to address social and environmental damage. The sieges paralyzed Chevron/Texaco's operations, costing them millions of dollars before a settlement was reached. Although this particular effort had only temporary impacts, it did contribute to shifting the dynamics and the narrative in the region, and the women remembered the power they collectively had been able to wield. A spokeswoman for the protesters said, "History has been made. Our culture is a patriarchal society. For women to come out like this and achieve what we have is out of the ordinary."

In Liberia in 2003, it was women's groups that led the Liberian Mass Action for Peace, finally stopping an incredibly brutal war that had decimated their nation for years. This historic coalition of Muslim and Christian women sat in public protest, confronted their nation's ruthless president and rebel warlords, and even, Lysistrata-like, held a sex strike to stop the violence. Subsequently, they elected a woman president from among their ranks. When women enter government in large enough numbers, studies show, in many cases the economy, the ecology and the general welfare in a country benefit, and a country tends to become less aggressive in its foreign policy. Much of this work begins with community organizing and brokering collaboration across differences at the grassroots, just as it did in Liberia.

More familiar to many is the example of the Green Belt Movement in Kenya, led by the late Wangari Maathai, who received a Nobel Peace Prize for her work. Not only did her organization plant over 51 million trees, but under her leadership the movement recognized and addressed the profound interconnectedness of environmental restoration to sustainability, democracy and the empowerment of women and girls.

In India, grassroots women's movements are breaking out all over. With help from a group called the Deccan Development Society, village women in Andhra Pradesh set up community grain and seed banks to gain control over their land, their food and their lives. By growing mainly food crops and managing the collection and disbursement of seeds, women have been achieving "intellectual leadership" in their villages. Working together through local village-level groups, the women form markets of their own, establishing prices that reflect their own needs and priorities. Through a government program that aims to rejuvenate marginalized lands, the women brought 2,500

acres of fallow land under cultivation. The sorghum they produced in
the first year of the project provided 3 million meals for 30 villages, or
1,000 extra meals per family. In each of 30 villages, the fodder from
their fields fed 6,000 cattle and produced wages for 2,500 people.

Since the program emphasizes reintroducing biodiversity and
the restoration of traditional crop varieties, lands that used to produce
crops worth 250–300 rupees per acre are now producing food crops
worth 4,000 rupees per acre. In two years 500 women have recovered
50 traditional crop varieties and set up banks for traditional seeds
in 30 villages. Renowned seed activist Vandana Shiva launched the
Navdanya movement, for farmers to retain control of their local food
supply and resist the co-opting of their native seeds and agriculture
by multinational agribusiness corporations. She has rallied millions to
take a stand. From India also, the legendary activist Medha Patkar and
writer and activist Arundhati Roy, among many others, helped mobilize
popular resistance against the dam-building policies of the Indian
government and the World Bank that displace millions of traditional
villagers while despoiling riparian ecosystems. These movements don't
always succeed, but even when they don't, they too leave seeds for the
next generations of women leaders to build upon.

These women-led movements often seek to solve several
interrelated problems simultaneously with a relational approach.
They seek to enhance local food security, resist corporate control and
pollution, increase local economic development and improve the overall
health of their communities.

Another hallmark of woman-led movements is the centrality
of coalition-building in their strategies. They often bring together
uncommon allies who can be made to see they share a common goal.
An interesting example of that approach can be found here in the U.S.

— a growing collaboration between reproductive rights activists and environmentalists around the issue of the proliferation of endocrine-disrupting chemicals in our environment and bodies. Linked to sterility and deformed genitalia in the offspring of fish and birds, ecologists had been sounding the alarm about the potential risks of these compounds for years, but once reproductive health activists understood the magnitude of the threat to human fertility and women's reproductive health, they began to understand the inexorable connection between the health of the environment and human health.

After struggling for over 30 years to preserve women's right to choose, reproductive rights organizations had become known for their fierce independence and narrow focus, rarely aligning with other issues or movements. Yet both communities recognized that peoples' ability to have healthy babies, the increasingly early onset of puberty in girls, and reproductive cancers in women were all at least partially linked to environmental factors, and both groups understood that this is something a powerful movement could be built upon. Surveys reflect that one of the greatest environmental concerns in opinion polling is chemical toxins, and anxiety is heightened when the worries are linked to reproductive impacts like decreased fertility or birth defects. A serious collaboration between these two groups of unlikely partners could succeed in bringing this issue far greater public attention — and in putting a human face on this huge environmental health concern.

In the last few decades it has become crystal-clear that what is good for women is good for the Earth. When women's equality, literacy and socio-economic power increase, women consistently choose to have fewer children (the difference between a woman with no schooling and 12 years of schooling is almost 4 to 5 children per woman). A study by the Worldwatch Institute finds that the only

proven, sure-fire way to reduce fertility rates and slow burgeoning
population growth in the global south is to give girls access to
education, end the rampant violence against women, and empower
women in every sphere of society.

Family planning has huge ripple effects in decreasing greenhouse
gas emissions. According to Project Drawdown, a research compilation
of one hundred ways to fight climate change by lowering atmospheric
CO^2, the total reduction of 119.2 gigatons that could result from
empowering and educating women and girls makes this an unexpected
top-tier solution to reversing global warming!

Climate change action at the grassroots is thus another huge
potential arena for coalition building among previously separate
organizations. I am very excited about two such recent coalitions
between Indigenous networks and climate activism: Indigenous Climate
Action and It Takes Roots.

Indigenous Climate Action, founded in 2015 in Alberta by five
Indigenous women leaders, strives to fill the gaps between the lived
experiences of Indigenous Peoples and the policies and strategies being
developed to address climate change. They support increasing climate
change literacy and the creation of a network for Indigenous climate
action that supports Indigenous water protectors, land defenders and
knowledge holders. Its first director is Eriel Deranger, a passionately
fierce organizer, wife and mother, who is a member of the Athabasca
Chipewyan First Nation. Her peoples's land was at the site of the
Alberta Tar Sands, so she's experienced firsthand the devastation that
has been brought upon her peoples's lifeways, health and culture, as well
as on their land and water.

It Takes Roots is a multiracial effort led by women and gender-
oppressed people of color and Indigenous people on the frontlines of

racial, housing and climate justice across the country. It is the result of years of relationship building across the Climate Justice Alliance, the Grassroots Global Justice Alliance, the Indigenous Environmental Network and the Right to the City Alliance alongside the Center for Story-based Strategy and the Ruckus Society. Together these national alliances represent 150 organizations in 30 states nationwide and in Canada. Each of these alliances is led by grassroots organizations, and each brings unique contributions to their collective work: strategies for a just transition to a regenerative economy; connections with global movements and grassroots feminist and gender justice organizations; a strong framework of environmental justice, Indigenous sovereignty and treaty rights; and deep experience in housing and land rights. This extraordinary coalition beautifully illustrates what the ecologically literate have long known: Just as all our problems are interrelated, so our solutions need to be interwoven as well.

As the late, often-prescient social analyst and pioneer of eco-psychology Theodore Roszak noted, as women's perspectives and voices are increasingly represented in leadership throughout all sectors, not only will gender equity become the norm, but the qualities that we have long associated as stereotypically "feminine" will grow to be more widely appreciated in everyone and in all organizations. The human capacities for caring, empathy, listening and compassion — which have so long been associated with mothers, nurses, caregivers and wives — will become fully embedded in our social values. Those social institutions that have previously been predicated upon competitive and aggressive market values will give increasing priority to cooperation, relational intelligence and caring. In the time ahead, we can anticipate that our social and cultural styles will be steadily reinvented and reshaped by the 51% of the world that's female. As proclaimed on placards at the immense Women's March in Washington, DC, following the 2017 presidential inauguration: *The Future is Female.*

In these, and many other emerging grassroots women-led movements here in the U.S. and around the world, we are seeing the seeds of Roszak's prediction, outlines of the coalitions we will need to cultivate, and the creative models we can begin to draw upon to develop an Earth-honoring, life-affirming culture.

RECLAIMING ACTIVISM

Indigeneity, Leadership
and Collaboration

(Interview with Ayana Young, *For the Wild*)

A yana Young is in service to the redwoods, to the salmon, to the whole wild Pacific Northwest ecosystems that seem to have spawned her and call her kin. She is deeply aligned with Indigenous culture-bearers and aware of how Indigeneity can and will affect movements to come. She conducts deep and insightful interviews on her podcast, *For The Wild*, seeking to illuminate the nexus between people and wildlands, between heart, spirit and action. I found her capacity to light up the connective tissue among seemingly disparate elements inspiring and particularly conducive to the leadership from the heart that's so needed in this pivotal and dangerous time.

Ayana Young: The environmental movements have historically been on separate tracks than human rights or women's movements, but in this time of convergent crises, it's undeniable that these challenges are inseparable, and just as corporate polluters are merging, the resistance must also merge. Bioneers has been instrumental in connecting these movements and showing how the environmental movement really must broaden its aims to remain relevant. Could you speak about how your ideas about activism as a holistic endeavor have evolved through the years at Bioneers, and would you share some of those connections you draw between issues of ecology and race, class and gender disparities?

Nina Simons: When we first started Bioneers, I didn't consider myself an activist. I considered myself a communicator and a producer, but I thought of activism in a very prescribed way, as people who demonstrated and got arrested or did direct actions. And those were not forms of activism that I was readily called toward.

Over the years, my exposure to Bioneers and all the diverse leaders that we have featured there really helped me to broaden my understanding of what activism can be. I've come to understand that there are as many ways to respond to the multiple interdependent crises and challenges we face as there probably are human beings on the planet. I now see communication absolutely as a form of activism, but so is raising children, and so is being a teacher, or a hospice worker, or a politician or policy maker. That's how Bioneers has helped me redefine activism as a holistic endeavor.

Drawing some of the connections between ecology, race, class, and gender...I had this sequential awakening about how all those other ways that we divide up human beings relate to our ecological crises. I think one of our first big "ahas" with Bioneers was perceiving the degree of factionalism that existed even within an environmental movement that, as you mentioned, was historically predominately white and mostly middle class, but yet still wildly divided within itself.

At Bioneers we sometimes refer to Indigenous people as not only the first Bioneers but as the old growth cultures who live among us. That began an awakening for me around history and racial justice. Then, the more that I got to know and hear people of all colors and classes speak, the more I understood the degree to which our culture operates in a hierarchical paradigm that tends to devalue and diminish the voices of people of color, people of lower income, and women as well.

AY: I'm wondering what you see as the barriers to embracing direct action on a larger scale, or at least supporting that as an individual or as a group?

NS: If I were to hazard a guess, I think the barriers are numerous and probably different for each individual. There's a barrier that has to do with the simple fact of self-preservation and a fear of putting oneself in harm's way.

We also have a lot of conditioning, depending on who we are. As a woman of Jewish lineage, I have identified conditioning in myself that has caused me in the past to try to smooth over ruptures that occur about racial difference and even the discomfort of sitting with another's trauma or pain. That tendency toward avoidance or pacifying has required me to intentionally build some courage and muscle in myself on a psychological level to be able to keep turning towards the discomfort of addressing those systems. I've had to keep asking "How do I develop my own capacity to stay in that conversation so that I can act on behalf of the world I want?"

We have been societally conditioned to be individualistic, and our solitary orientation gives us little practice at, and few tools for, acting collectively. Even in the formation of our movements we tend toward competition and factionalism, and we're not yet skillful or practiced at collaborating together toward greater impacts.

AY: As North Dakota militarizes its response to the Standing Rock protest, the racial injustices that the tribes have suffered for centuries are being brought again into the spotlight. Even today, poverty, incarceration and unemployment rates among Native Americans in North Dakota are some of the highest in the country. For the first time in modern history, we see 200 Indigenous nations uniting to protect water and their role as Earth guardians. Do you believe the climate movement will continue moving towards uplifting Indigenous priorities, perspectives and leadership, and how would that benefit the movement?

NS: I'm not 100 percent sure that the climate movement will ally itself with Indigenous justice movements, but I sure am throwing everything I know or have in that direction. So, I hope it will. I pray it will. And I'm doing everything I can to help it align in that way.

I think that there are a number of large-scale movements that are orienting increasingly towards honoring the role of First Nations as leaders of the climate movement. To be honest, we're going to need so many leaders, and leaders of all colors and of all ages. I think that leadership is emergent on many fronts right now.

What's happening at Standing Rock is simultaneously incredibly exciting and deeply tragic, as you say. The militarized response is not dissimilar to what has happened at other Native uprisings that have occurred in the past, but the advent of social media and of some independent media sources like Democracy Now! is making it harder for repression to happen in a way that's invisible to the larger public. I think the visibility of the violent, orchestrated response is a tremendous help to our movements.

In addition to the representatives of more than 200 sovereign Indigenous nations there at Standing Rock, there are a great many non-native people there too, and to me that's part of what's most exciting about what's happening. There is an openness and receptivity, in spite of all the history that tells Native people to be mistrustful of non-native allies; this continued receptivity and welcoming and true generosity of spirit that's welcoming the non-native allies who are showing up there is remarkable and could augur well for future coalition building.

I believe that Native people have an essential role in leading the climate revolution that is to come, but of course it's not only a climate revolution, as you point out, it's about water, it's about clean air, it's about the future of our children, and it's about the future of ourselves as a species, to be blunt. It's also about rebelling against the corporate state, which in many ways is what makes Standing Rock different than past Native stands, because in the past it was governments who were quashing Native rebellions. This time it's banks and corporations backed by governments that are behind the violence that's happening there.

My hope and prayer is that the visibility of Indigenous and Aboriginal peoples leading this movement of movements will help translate into a shift in our worldview. There are ways that I keep learning from Indigenous friends and acquaintances the depth of how they relate to every aspect of life around us as a living relation, filled with consciousness and spirit.

At a gathering that I attended to strengthen efforts to protect the Bears Ears as a national monument, there was an eloquent Lakota man named Tiokasin Ghosthorse who broadcasts First Voices Indigenous Radio out of New York's WBAI. We were doing a soil ceremony, and he said, "In my language, the word we use to describe soil means 'Who we used to be.'"

I thought that was such a profound way of invoking the longer timeframe that many Indigenous people live with, the recognition that the soil is who we used to be and that we will go back to being soil after our brief experience in human form on this planet. It's a whole different kind of perspective and respect of relational intelligence than our Western culture has been raised to recognize, so my hope is that Indigenous peoples' centrality to this movement will help accelerate cultural shifts and a real transformation in worldview that's so needed right now.

AY: As you've alluded to, generosity and mutual aid characterize many Indigenous societies around the world, but in capitalist societies where greed is rewarded, sacrifice is almost nonsensical. It's a major hurdle to overcome, this aversion to sacrifice, and it prevents people from making substantial commitments to positive change. You've spent much of your life in service, and I'd love to hear from your point of view, what would be needed for us as a society to shift towards a culture of simplicity and service, to overcome our energy-intense lifestyles, to break that inertia?

NS: Thank you for asking big questions that push me to venture deep inside myself to see how I'm going to respond. One of the things that my own life has brought me to is an inquiry around how we are reinventing leadership in this time, because I realized that what was most needed from everyone was leadership, and that our inherited model of leadership was not one that many people I knew (including myself) could wholeheartedly embrace.

One of the complex parts of our inherited model that I've grappled with is the question of sacrifice. When I first started looking at it, I thought, why does leadership necessarily have to involve sacrifice? Maybe that's part of the old paradigm; maybe it doesn't have to involve sacrifice.

Now, when I look back at the "me" who asked that question, I have to chuckle because of her naïveté, because life has taught me that sacrifice is often integral to real leadership. As an example, Kenny and I — Kenny is my husband and partner with whom I co-founded Bioneers — ran Bioneers for eight years with almost no compensation, basically doing it in our spare time on top of our day jobs. We did it because we loved it. We did it because it felt really important and necessary to us. We certainly didn't do it for personal gain. At the end of those eight years, we were exhausted, so it was kind of a sacrifice right from the beginning, but of course compared to the sacrifices of so many people around the world in far more challenging environments, it was not that traumatic, and we ultimately reaped great rewards for doing it.

Part of what's needed, I think, is new models of leadership, and one of the things that's important to helping shift our culture is to see examples of leaders who have embraced leadership in a wholehearted way and who have made their peace with sacrifice as a part of that, but who still exude joy and who live balanced lives and take care of themselves as well as others. There's an old mental model of a sort of heroic leadership that fetishizes tireless effort. We need a new model of leadership that integrates all of our human capacities and qualities. That means being vulnerable enough to say, "There's a lot of blood, sweat and tears that went into my work, but it has led to some of the most rewarding moments in my life, and I would not retrace my steps and undo those risks or those sacrifices for any amount of money."

Part of the answer to your question lies also in lifting up role models of all races and backgrounds and ages and genders so that we can all see the plethora of options that are open to us and recognize that there are elements of working for the common good that provide a level of meaning and fulfillment that outweigh any monetary gain. One guiding principle in my life comes from a quote by the Austrian physicist Fritjof Capra. He said that the shift to an eco-literate society, a society that knows how to live in right relationship to nature, involves a shift from an emphasis on counting and accumulating things to an emphasis on mapping relationships — from quantity to quality, from a goal orientation to one that's much more process-oriented.

One of the ways I believe we can shift from this egocentric, greed-centric culture to one that is more collaboratively, communally oriented is to focus on relationships as the things that give us the greatest meaning in our lives, and not just relationships within the human world but to the more-than-human world — to the elements, to the ancestors, to the plants and animals and fungi upon which our lives depend.

AY: Thank you, Nina, for sharing those thoughts and some of your personal sacrifices. It's a question I've been thinking about for a while as I moved onto raw land a little over two years ago, living in a tent through very rainy winters, and tried to look deeply into what is actually fulfilling, as we move through this extremely over-consumptive system. What does real purpose feel like, and how can we actually reciprocate and sacrifice for what we love, the more-than-human world, as you so beautifully put it?

I think back to something you said earlier in the interview: it can

*sometimes be challenging for people who are interested in the same things
to really learn how to work together or even know of each other, and I'm
wondering, what are some ways that you're experiencing collaboration really
taking off, and what are some of the tools we can all keep in mind as we try
to build regenerative projects with others?*

NS: Honestly, I feel like I am in a process of trying to identify those
tools and really codify them so that they can be more accessible to all
of us, but one thing I would say is that intimate relationship is one of
the hardest spiritual practices — perhaps the hardest — that I have
encountered in my life. Anyone who is in a very long-term relationship,
who's paying attention, would likely agree. It's no accident that our
divorce rate is as high as it is because we get so little training in how to
be in effective, close, long-term relationships.

   Some of what I can suggest, Ayana, is that building
collaborative capacity takes time. It takes practice, just like anything
else. One of the principles that I have found really helpful (and this
has come out of our women's leadership work, but it's true for people
of any gender) is to prioritize relationship over task; to actually take
the time to really build relationship and to choose to share intimate
stories. They then help you understand why you may be coming
from different perspectives or disagree when you do because one of
our greatest challenges as human beings is that we tend to think that
people who think like us are smart, and people who don't think like us
are not. Because of that we tend to form into groups of like-minded
people. That is understandable but not very helpful for movement-
building or collaboration.

   One of the ideas that I have found as a countervailing force to
that tendency is the notion that comes from my friend and mentor

Jeannette Armstrong, who's an extraordinary First Nations educator
from the Okanagan people in British Columbia. In her tradition, they
practice something called the Four Societies or E'Nowkin Weh. In
that tradition, what they say is that the most valuable perspective that
anyone can bring is one that's 180 degrees opposed from my own,
because that requires me to be able to expand my thinking and my
vision enough to incorporate their perspective. Wow, how would the
world be different if we all practiced that.

So, the clearest offerings I can respond with are to suggest
prioritizing relationship ahead of task, to give time and space for that
relationship to evolve and mature, to recognize that partnership or
collaboration is a practice, and to make some agreements about what
happens when you don't agree, and what happens when you might
inadvertently trigger an emotional response in someone else, and how
are you going to deal with that.

If you talk about those things at the front end and make
some agreements about them, that can really help, because those
eruptions often happen, and they occur not by intention but
because privilege comes with blinders, and we often don't know
another's reality enough to be able to avoid offending them, so
we inadvertently say or do things that offend, and if we know in
advance and we've talked about the likelihood that that might
happen, we might make agreements that could include how we
name it when something like that happens and how we agree to
respond to it. Do we take a break for a time and then re-meet to
try to unpack what happened? What is our commitment about how
we're going to move through difficult challenges?

Another of the guiding principles that's been really helpful to
me comes from a mentor named Dawna Markova. She says that the

durability, flexibility and resilience of relationships are a function of how we navigate rupture and repair. All our relationships, whether they're parent/child or sibling or partner or colleague or friend or life partner, all of our relationships will encounter ruptures. When the rupture happens, it's whether and how we choose to turn back towards repair that confers strength and endurance to our relationships.

AY: Thank you so much. You were expressing at the beginning the value of really being able to commit to sit in the discomfort sometimes and not running away, and I know a lot of that's come up with racial justice issues and white privilege. If we give space and give time and love and dedication and commitment, we can come through these messy growing pains and learn to work together in a new regenerative way.

ILLUMINATING POSSIBILITIES

Leaders Lifting Others Up

I'd like to describe a few of my many sheroes, women leading innovative change whose stories show just how diverse are the paths and options toward emergent, love-inspired leadership, and what a wide array of methods and approaches women leaders choose. Their stories illustrate the movement from inner guidance, love or prompting to outer expression, and their many accomplishments as innovators and cultural or ecological healers are mirrored by their embodiment of values I hold most dear: deep listening, embodied connectedness, relational intelligence, a passion for justice held within healing, reverence for nature, joy, creativity, a sense of the sacred and celebration. Many of them also lead by creating events, forums and conditions for others to flourish and emerge as leaders. For those, leadership is defined by how many others they can lift up. These women have augmented my learning, and many others are profiled in *Moonrise: The Power of Women Leading from the Heart*, which shares stories of many more of my earlier mentors and role models.

KATSI COOK

There is a saying about the Iroquois or Haudenosaunee Six Nations: "If you want something done, get a Mohawk to do it." There is no better living proof of that than Katsi Cook. A member of the Mohawk Nation, one of the Iroquois Six Nations Confederacy, she commits herself unerringly and with great love toward unleashing the potential that exists within the North American Indigenous world.

After decades of connecting people, purpose and initiatives, she is renowned especially for two immense contributions: she has been the most important visionary leader in the revitalization of traditional Native American midwifery, and is one of the earliest and most influential researchers on environmental health impacts on Indigenous people.

It all starts with Katsi herself. A mother of five and grandmother of 11, she exudes a healing, nurturing aura and a quality of being that's grounded in vibrant family and community, which feeds her seemingly endless energy.

Katsi has profoundly affirmed the value for women of reinhabiting our bodies, listening and learning from our inherent biological wisdom. Katsi's sense of embodiment is informed by her people's Longhouse tradition. "Women are the first environment," she says. "We are an embodiment of our Mother Earth. From the bodies of women flows the relationship of the generations both to society and the natural world. With our bodies we nourish, sustain and create connected relationships and interdependence. In this way, the Earth is our mother, our ancestors said. In this way, we as women are Earth."

When she began witnessing the profound effects upon women's health of toxins in the water, she shifted her focus to initiate the famous Akwesasne Mother's Milk Project, which launched highly influential studies on PCB and heavy metals contamination in her community. As a community organizer, and natural networker, Katsi's commitment to Indigenous peoples has led her to be widely known throughout the hundreds of tribal nations and communities that comprise Indian Country. She has sought out and connected with grassroots and community leaders whether they are known to mainstream culture or not. Thanks to her influence, I now have a greater appreciation for the leaders who often fly under the radar, who are not necessarily represented as leaders of stature in the media but are deeply respected and valued in their own communities.

And as is true for so many women leaders who become drawn toward new or later-in-life callings, her path has evolved into new ways to serve her community, now as the Director of the Spirit Aligned Leadership Program. There, she is convening an Inaugural Circle of eight Indigenous Elder women who will together inform future circles and approaches "so that what lives deep within our Indigenous girls and women and Mother Earth can connect and come forth now in these extremely critical times." Because I see Indigenous women and the traditional cultural values and knowledge ways they carry as holding the key to all women's — and all peoples' — survival, this most recent expression of her work thrills me to the core, and offers tremendous promise as a strategic investment in our collective future.

LENY MENDOZA STROBEL

I first met Leny when she participated in one of the trainings I was leading, and as sometimes happens, we became fast friends. This elegant, sophisticated and dignified professor, Chair of the Department of American Multicultural Studies at Sonoma State University, impressed me with her clarity and directness about colonialism's impacts, the beauty of her Filipino Indigenous culture, and her profound insights about the value of multiculturalism.

I soon discovered that in addition to having written three wonderful books (*A Book of Her Own* is perhaps the best book I've ever seen that describes in detail how to "decolonize" one's mind), she was also the Project Director of the Center for Babaylan Studies, which works to help Filipinos around the world and is dedicated to the twin goals of decolonization and indigenization.

From Leny's endlessly curious and open mind and heart I have learned about opening to new people and ideas while staying purposefully and with great integrity on path. When she invited me to speak at her university to a class on multiculturalism, I realized that — in addition to living in a California county that's predominantly white, the students that this radically committed woman worked with on a daily basis came mostly from very privileged, white homes, and had little embodied experience — beyond her teachings — of the value of multiculturalism. Her dedication to teaching with deep respect — both toward her students, but especially to benefit other Filipino immigrants — is unflagging in spite of facing challenging odds and a pervasively unsupportive environment.

Perhaps more than anything, Leny embodies the integration — gleaned from her own arduous work at self-reclamation — of the values of her Indigenous roots. In her books she explains her discovery process, illuminating pathways for others to follow her self-decolonization efforts. She manages to bridge her Indigenous inner world with the modern Western world she has to live and work in with an elegant balance of humility and great dignity.

Leny (born Elenita) has produced cutting-edge curricula, conferences, books and webinars that create pathways of healing for people of all cultures, but especially those of the Filipino diaspora. Filipinos suffered enormous hardships in several wars in the 20th century, and many who had to migrate to survive had their labor ruthlessly exploited in many countries. They have had very few champions, but they can be very proud to have produced as impeccable and luminous a leader, teacher and defender as Leny Mendoza Strobel.

JULIA BUTTERFLY HILL

It may sound like a cliché, but Julia Butterfly Hill really is a force of nature. She is best known for having lived in a 180-foot tall, roughly 1,500-year-old California redwood tree for over two years — for 738 days — between December 10, 1997 and December 18, 1999. Julia climbed that tree, which she lovingly named Luna, when she was 23 years old, to prevent Pacific Lumber Company loggers from cutting it down.

While living in Luna, Julia learned many survival skills, such as seldom washing the soles of her feet, because the sap helped her feet stick to the branches better. With ropes, she hoisted up survival supplies brought by an eight-member support crew and to keep warm, she wrapped herself tightly into a sleeping bag, leaving only a small hole for breathing. She used solar-powered cell phones for radio interviews, became an "in-tree" correspondent for a cable television show, and hosted TV crews to protest old-growth clear-cutting.

During her ordeal, Julia weathered freezing rains and high winds, helicopter harassment, a ten-day siege by company security guards and attempted intimidation by angry loggers. A resolution was reached in 1999 when the Pacific Lumber Company agreed to preserve Luna and all trees within a 200-foot buffer zone. In exchange, Julia agreed to vacate the tree.

I first met Julia virtually, by audio only, when she spoke at Bioneers from her perch in Luna. We were able to pipe her into our conference in San Francisco, and as her voice rang out with all the love, anger, pain, reverence and commitment that coursed through her, chills ran up and down my spine. When she spoke of how sacred the old growth forest is to her, and her reverent relationship to Luna, she moved everyone to tears.

So, it's no wonder that since her tree sit, Hill has become a motivational speaker, a bestselling author, and the co-founder of the Circle of Life Foundation and the Engage Network, a nonprofit that trains small groups of civic leaders to work toward social change. She is the author of the book, *The Legacy of Luna*, and co-author of *One Makes the Difference*. More recently, Julia has also become a proponent of tax redirection, resisting payment of about $150,000 in federal taxes and instead donating that money to afterschool programs, arts and cultural programs, community gardens, alternatives to incarceration and environmental protection programs.

When, some years after her tree sit, Julia spoke in person at our conference, she noticed how few young people were there. She responded by helping to initiate the Bioneers Youth Program. She turned to me and Kenny backstage and said "There aren't enough young people out there. Do you want me to help?" And of course we said "Yes!" This is another quality I've witnessed about feminine leadership: the ability to respond in the moment without questioning the impulse or doubting one's ability to act. Julia trusts her own inner voice, and she just exudes natural spiritual authority because of it. I reflect now upon her actions with tremendous gratitude, and part of her legacy is that more than 500 young people now attend our youth program each year.

LILY YEH

Lily Yeh, with immense courage, opted to shift her professional course after becoming well established in her field, due to a soul calling, or change of heart. An artist who grew up in Taiwan and later moved to the United States, she worked as a professor of painting and art history at the University of the Arts in Philadelphia for thirty years. By all external measures, she had succeeded at all the "normal" things, like family and work, but this outer success had not fulfilled her. It hadn't given her an authentic sense of purpose. She was to find that purpose when one day she was invited to a traumatized, poverty-stricken part of Philadelphia, a neighborhood she didn't normally visit. She felt a sudden urge to help co-create an art piece in this challenging environment. She invited residents to join her in creating a large mosaic out of the shards of broken glass in an empty lot. Soon the word got out, and Lily's magnetic personality drew people in: local kids and their parents, homeless folks, even street hustlers, all became collaborators in what would become the most important art project of her life. The whole neighborhood became engaged in cleaning up

the area, painting murals, and creating an "art park." Soon, it became
The Village of Arts and Humanities, which yearly serves over 10,000
low-income, primarily African American youth and families, covering
several neighborhoods within a nearly three-hundred-square block
area in North Philadelphia. Lily witnessed the power of collaborative
art to help create new bonds among members of a hitherto neglected
community. As its founder and executive director, Lily had created a
national model in creative "place-making" and community-building
through the arts, but she did not rest there.

When she heard a man from Rwanda speaking about the
devastating genocide that had ripped apart his country, she said: "My
heart moved, and I responded." With just $5,000 in her pocket, she
went to Rwanda and accompanied him to a village where hundreds
of traumatized survivors lived. There she helped create a collaborative
mosaic memorial chamber for the bones of the murdered. Not only
did this activity help knit the community together, the memorial
project helped foster other development, including animal husbandry
initiatives, a sewing business run by orphans, a traditional basket
weaving cooperative, and the training of solar engineers so that now
every home has solar energy. She trusted her heart's and intuition's
guidance, and with the village in collaboration, a memorial art piece set
in motion a whole cascade of locally empowering projects.

In 2002, Lily founded Barefoot Artists, Inc., and she has since
helped launch arts projects in countries all over the world, including
Kenya, Ecuador, Syria, China, Haiti, India, Taiwan and Palestine. Lily
is always scared when she starts a project, but she starts anyway. Her
tiny delicate body contains tremendous courage. Now in her 70s, she is
doing what she feels she was born to do, with quiet dignity, following
her inner instructions. This has given her an incredibly luminous aura:

people everywhere are drawn to her; they just want to work with her. Her passion is contagious and transformational. She follows her muse and her inner spirit, not letting fear deter her, and as a result she has brought hope and healing to dozens of traumatized communities around the world.

FANIA DAVIS

Fania Davis grew up in Birmingham, Alabama and experienced firsthand the impacts of the violence that accompanied the movement to end segregation and racism. When she was 15, two of her close friends were killed in the infamous Birmingham Sunday School bombing carried out by white supremacists. Only six years later, her husband was shot and nearly killed by police because of their activism at the time in support of the Black Panthers. In her early twenties, she devoted herself to getting a law degree and organizing an international movement to defend her sister, Angela Davis, from politically motivated capital murder charges aimed at silencing her calls for racial and social justice. These experiences set her on a quest for social transformation, and for the following several decades, Fania was active in many movements for justice.

As a civil rights trial lawyer, Fania spent much of her professional life protecting people from racial discrimination, but after more than three decades of relentless fighting, she started to feel out of balance. She intuitively knew she needed more healing energies in her life. Like so many women I deeply admire, her path kept evolving as she responded to changing inner and outer realities. She ended up enrolling in a Ph.D. program in Indigenous Studies that allowed her to study

Indigenous cultures and apprentice with traditional African healers. This opened up a whole new world of deeper knowledge and experience that ignited a new phase of her activism. Fania then went on to become a radical innovator in social healing. Realizing from her work in the trenches how deeply flawed our criminal justice system is, Fania was inspired by South Africa's Truth and Reconciliation Commission and New Zealand's juvenile justice reforms to found Restorative Justice for Oakland Youth, RJOY, in 2005.

RJOY has been getting exceptionally positive results in the Oakland public school system and is becoming a luminous model for the rest of the country. Fania's concerns extend beyond establishing restorative justice in the human realm. She has come to understand that the rights of the natural world need be central in order for human psyches to be healed. She has become one of the key thought leaders in the emerging field of Restorative Justice in law schools and universities. A grandmother of three, Fania continues to practice law in Oakland, but she is also a dancer and a yoga and qigong practitioner. To be in her presence is to bask in beauty, serenity and grace. While her journey has changed course many times, she has always stayed true to serving the communities and people she loves. This is a woman who has learned to listen attentively for inner guidance and to adjust her approach. This has enabled her to help not only individual people in their quests for justice but to go deeper to seek to transform the very systems that perpetuate injustice. She has the remarkable capacity to inspire and lift up those she works with and for, cultivating leadership in everyone around her. She is one of the most impeccable and effective change agents I have ever met as well as one of the most balanced and serenely luminous women on the planet.

TAIJ KUMARIE MOTEELALL

An Indo-Caribbean artist and activist, Taij applied to come to one of our Cultivating Women's Leadership intensives, noting that she was still nursing her first child. She also asked whether she could bring her husband along to help care for the baby. She had formerly been Executive Director of Resource Generation, a network in which she'd worked with young people with wealth to help them align their values with their philanthropic giving and optimally organize and leverage their capacity as change-makers. We recognized the daunting challenges motherhood can pose and we really admired Taij's work and her achievements, so we were conflicted and unsure what to do. After lengthy consideration, we decided it simply wouldn't be fair to the other women, as we had never had any men present at the trainings. We apologetically informed her of our decision, but she was undaunted. With perseverance and determination, which I've since learned is typical of her, she reapplied the following year. She attended, and we became friends, and we have collaborated in varying ways ever since.

Taij is the founder and network weaver of Standing in Our Power, an intergenerational network of women of color leaders. Previously, she cofounded Media Sutra, a strategic consulting company that supports individuals and organizations to be more effective and sustainable as they seek to have a positive social impact and move people to action. Deeply connected to her roots, she also cofounded Jahajee Sisters, a movement-building organization that supports the leadership development of Indo-Caribbean women organizing against gender-based oppression and violence.

Standing in Our Power (SiOP) began with an initial gathering in 2012 and then kicked off a 10-month Transformational Leadership

Institute (TLI) with a national retreat in October 2013. The institute included local and national gatherings, coaching, training and mentoring. A Women of Color in Philanthropy initiative began in 2014, and in 2016 SiOP began partnering with foundations to offer capacity-building services and transformational leadership development programs to their grantees. SiOP is also preparing to launch a Women of Color Business Incubator. It's extraordinary how many potentially groundbreaking initiatives Taij has launched and sustained in the last few years.

Taij braids together multiple commitments: to motherhood, to creating pathways for women of color in leadership across multiple disciplines and sectors, to her own health and self-care, and to the arts and spirituality that are foundational to her core being. If she weren't busy enough, she is also working on a book about her Indo-Caribbean heritage and immigrant experience. She inspires me with her vision, her tireless but balanced energy, and her extraordinary capacity to bring new organizations and programs into form. I sometimes see her as the embodiment of a beneficent, twirling, many-armed goddess who generates positive outcomes as she dances through the world.

AI-JEN POO

Ai-jen Poo has been organizing immigrant women workers since 1996. The daughter of pro-democracy activists who emigrated from Taiwan, she felt called to work for those who help raise our children and care for the ill and elderly, without whom many families would be unable to function. Until recently these people who are so essential to our families and communities have labored incredibly long hours under appalling conditions with almost no protections or rights, no overtime, no health insurance, and no safety net. Watching her grandfather deteriorate in a nursing home but finding a good caregiver for her grandmother, she experienced firsthand the impact that a good caregiver had on her entire family's life, but she knew that domestic work is among the most underappreciated forms of labor in our society.

"What," she asks, "could be more important than caring for the people who care for us? It's the kind of job that's not even seen as a real job. Domestic workers and caregivers go to work every day and support the dignity and wellbeing of others. There is something uniquely human about caring and doing for others," she declares.

By mobilizing caregivers to fight to improve the systems that support them, she's taking a stand on behalf of the nurturing and relational part of our humanity, and seeking to transform core aspects of our culture. She has had very large-scale successes and gained a lot of national recognition for her organizing and advocacy work, but she remains consistently humble, caring and receptive herself, modeling the kind of care she's defending.

She is a remarkably skilled organizer who has been successful in helping large groups of some of the most disenfranchised people in our society achieve dignity and a better life. She has been able to help incorporate new constituencies into the labor movement and to build broad, effective coalitions and alliances. In 2000, she helped start Domestic Workers United (DWU), a New York-based organization that spearheaded the passage of the state's historic Domestic Workers Bill of Rights, which in turn helped lead to the creation of the National Domestic Workers Alliance, an alliance of domestic workers in 19 cities and 11 states, working to gain respect, recognition, and legal protections for America's 2.5 million domestic workers.

Ai-jen then helped launch the visionary "Caring Across Generations" campaign that seeks to unite mostly immigrant home-care workers with the increasing number of elders needing care as the baby boom generation ages. If these two very different groups could recognize their common interest in creating a healthy, well-regulated home-care sector that provides decent wages and high quality care, then, Ai-jen figured, a powerful, mutually beneficial movement that protects the rights of immigrant workers, provides good jobs, and offers excellent healthcare for the young and the elderly could coalesce and help address a number of our most pressing social problems. This is truly a stroke of political genius and "whole systems thinking."

Ai-jen radiates both profound compassion and a burning desire for fairness. The way she sees leadership is that her role is fundamentally to mobilize resources and people to achieve a positive social goal. She does that as effectively and graciously as anyone I've ever seen in action, because it's obvious that all her work is based in genuine love. She exquisitely balances humility, self-respect and dignity, and as a result she creates communities of respect and right relationship around her. As I've learned how hard it can be to reach that equilibrium and maintain it, my respect and admiration for her has grown exponentially over the years.

Recently, she took a sabbatical and spent four months re-energizing in Hawaii, in "places where mountains and ocean meet," where she spent time alone practicing yoga and sleeping at least eight hours each night, which she had rarely been able to do for years. In this, she modeled what so many women leaders need — an ongoing attention to exquisite self-care. So many of us desperately need to interrupt patterns of nonstop work that inevitably lead to burn-out. We have to learn to care lovingly for our bodies as the vehicles for our leadership, as much as we care for the communities, lands and places we are seeking to serve. In this aspect of life too, Ai-jen is offering us an example to emulate, if we want to be around and effective for the long haul.

JUDY WICKS

The most joyful and innovative businessperson I know, Judy Wicks brings unparalleled exuberance and celebration to business. She reinvented her successful restaurant enterprise repeatedly over the course of several decades. She took a restaurant and made it not only an extraordinary eatery but a groundbreaking vehicle for education and consciousness raising, as well as a catalyst to reknit the very social fabric of her community. Judy founded Philadelphia's White Dog Café, which became an early pioneer in the farm-to-table movement and a truly exemplary model of a sustainable and socially engaged business. Her other business practices that were far ahead of the curve included: paying a living wage, instituting fair-trade principles in her purchasing, stringently recycling and composting, using solar heating and eco-friendly cleaning products and office supplies, and purchasing 100 percent of her electricity from renewable sources (the very first business in Pennsylvania to do so). She even incorporated the mentoring of inner city high school students in her business model. Her restaurant may also be the only such establishment to have had a foreign policy: she led a number of tours to developing countries, including Cuba, to study sustainable agro-ecological practices, bolster fair trade relationships, and enhance international and cross-cultural understanding.

When she tried something new that worked, she shared it with her competitors in order to better transform the city. Judy mentored several generations of entrepreneurs in Philadelphia and well beyond. Before starting White Dog, Judy had had two other successful local businesses: Black Cat, which sold locally made and fair trade crafts and Free People Store which later became Urban Outfitters. She is also far more than a successful entrepreneur: she has been a thought leader in reimagining what business is and should be, as well as the types of economies local communities need to develop in order to thrive. She has absolute clarity about an economy's true purpose: maximizing relationships, not profits. She co-founded Fair Food Philly and the Sustainable Business Network of Greater Philadelphia and then went on to co-found the highly influential nationwide network BALLE, the Business Alliance for Local Living Economies. It started with the simple premise that an environmentally, socially, and financially sustainable global economy needs to be based on a network of sustainable local economies. BALLE's network has grown to over 80 local business networks in the U.S. and Canada that together include over 20,000 small businesses.

Judy recounted many of her adventures and ideas in her award-winning memoir *Good Morning, Beautiful Business*. Her achievements speak for themselves, but they are not what I admire most about Judy. In service to the well-being of her community, no political win or holiday goes without Judy spearheading a huge block party or some sort of celebration. For her, localization means collective joy at home, dancing in the street, balls and comedy skits and holiday festivities. She reminds me that personal fulfillment and pleasure are not only possible but essential along an activist path.

CLIMBING POETREE: ALIXA GARCIA AND NAIMA PENNIMAN

Every time I hear Climbing PoeTree perform, they enliven my heart, mind and soul. This spoken word duo — Alixa Garcia and Naima Penniman — elevate awareness and engagement through their intense open-heartedness, piercing intelligence, inspired writing, musical talent, impeccable performance skills and a luminous presence. They deliver some of the most radically awakening and uplifting socially "conscious" artistic performances anywhere, and they are both multifaceted in their creative endeavors: they are each award-winning multimedia artists, committed social justice activists, and professional educators. Their unshakeable integrity makes them insist on maintaining complete control over their artistic production and their appearances. They are bold cross-cultural experimenters who engage in what they call "international, bilingual, pansexual, poly-racial, multi-media, cross-genre, intergalactic collaborations."

They are true independents — women who would rather perform in a prison or a school in a disaster zone than on a reality TV show. They have performed at the notorious Riker's Island jail, as well as at such diverse venues as the Brooklyn Academy of Music, the UN, Harvard, and to benefit countless community-based organizations. They have independently self-organized 30 national and international tours, from South Africa to Cuba, from the United Kingdom to Mexico, and throughout the United States, including 11,000 miles touring on a bus with an all-woman crew and that was converted to run on recycled vegetable oil.

In one of their most remarkable initiatives, they collected over *six thousand* stories on square pieces of fabric and stitched them together into an ever-growing *tapestry of truth* that they use to lead workshops in high schools, colleges, and correctional institutions across the nation around the power of storytelling for movement building. They've also developed an arts-based curriculum to inspire the next generation of social change agents, a course being piloted in several high schools and universities in five states. They have organized solidarity work in Haiti bringing together artists, farmers and traditional healers to collaborate with a rural community to plant trees and share skills. They're also co-creating a transformative living center for women of color activist/artists to create, heal, garden, connect and flourish.

And in addition to all this extraordinary collaborative work, they each also pursue distinct solo professional and creative projects. Alixa's multi-dimensional, lucite-encased collage portraits of justice movement leaders, designed to be showcased accompanied by her audio interviews with them, are breathtaking, and Naima is also an accomplished visual artist. It is impossible not to be awed by these two women. Their uniquely powerful poetry can burn with the fire of justice and rage against oppression, but it can also be tender and loving and ever attentive to the sacredness of all life. The mainstream world may not know it, but they are the most gifted, potent and authentic poets of our era. They continue to inspire audiences around the country and the world toward greater engagement as they also co-create communities of leadership among a wide range of women artist/activists. Their creativity, passion, work ethic, wisdom, soulfulness, integrity and literary genius know no bounds, and their art and friendship consistently bring me to tears of joy and inspired glee.

JOANNA MACY

A widely beloved mentor to so many of us in this movement to
reconnect ourselves with Mother Earth, Joanna Macy is a wise elder,
environmental activist, author, and scholar. She is truly a unique figure,
one who in the course of her many decades of service has managed
to marry traditional Indigenous wisdom, "whole-systems" thinking,
Buddhist wisdom, Deep Ecology, empathic connection and engaged
action into a powerful, coherent, inspiring philosophical framework
— a compass for effective action and meaningful living. She teaches
through experience and example that love's power to transform our
world must be inextricably woven with our often less appreciated
emotions of outrage, grief and loss. She has understood more fully
than anyone that in order to be able to transform our world, we
need to embrace the full gamut of human emotions and rekindle
our connections to all of life, including our ancestors and our future
descendants.

Joanna became an internationally renowned activist in anti-
nuclear, peace, social justice, and environmental movements, and most
recently she created an initiative called "The Great Turning," which
maps in a profoundly sophisticated way how we can transform our
consciousness, so we can transition from our unsustainable, destructive
industrial society to a far more just and sane civilization. She also
developed an approach ("The Work that Reconnects") designed to help
people respond creatively to the global crises we face rather than feeling
overwhelmed or paralyzed.

Connecting with Joanna, experiencing her teachings and seeing
her example, helped me acknowledge the power of my own emotions,
especially my grief. She showed me that when we open our hearts to

the overwhelming suffering in our world, and we face that pain and
let ourselves grieve fully, we not only become more complete human
beings, we become far more effective at doing good, because we are then
able to place our own pain within a larger context that gives it meaning.
Rather than being afraid of our own emotions, they can become the
most powerful tools to re-enliven us, and, paradoxically, to help us
reconnect to our sense of joy. In this state our capacity to create change
dramatically increases.

Now in her eighties, Joanna continues to travel and give
lectures, workshops, and trainings internationally. Joanna reminds me
that transformative learning must reach our whole selves, including
our body, heart, mind and spirit, to be fully integrated. She has
long embodied the values of practice, lifelong learning, ceaseless
commitment, and the regenerative power of love. In her persevering
quest to develop tools for navigating the dire challenges we face as a
species, she has brilliantly woven together disparate strands of wisdom
to create unique, dynamic new systemic forms of learning. She has
shared them generously and tirelessly, and her legacy will live on far,
far beyond her lifetime, as the thousands of us she has inspired will
carry forward her transmitted teachings and pass them on in turn to
generations to come.

While hugely divergent in ethnicity, age, background, education
and form of expression, each of the leaders I have sought to describe
above embodies moving from inner authority and a sense of purpose
or love outward, into the world of action. They all seek to bring the
totality of themselves to their engagement with the challenges of our
era. They all practice deep listening to others and to their inner light for
guidance, know how to balance humility with self-respect and dignity,

and have honed the ability to respond spontaneously in the moment. Many are particularly skillful in seeing what the world needs and are joyous in fulfilling their unique purpose in service to it. Each also embodies a celebration of connection and an intimacy with the spiritual realms of life. It is my good fortune that through my work I have encountered so many of these extraordinary women who have taught me more than I could ever repay.

All are in their own ways, healers. Many are artists, creating new visions and possibilities as they innovate; and all are storytellers, as it is through changing the story, I believe, that we can change the world.

THE POWER OF STORY

...to reclaim our voices, express our truth, shed negative conditioning, find our life purpose, become who we yearn to be, awaken our vision, attract support, connect with allies, and mobilize change...

Women's oppression has been enabled, perpetuated and strengthened by silence, shame and isolation. When we contemplate the waves of women's liberation and rights movements over time and throughout different parts of the globe, we can see that they are always accompanied by women getting together and sharing their stories. It's only when we stop being silent and start to speak and make our voices heard that real change starts to happen. It is no exaggeration to say that when a woman speaks her truth, the world changes. As Ursula K. LeGuin, the late great poet and novelist, says: "We are volcanoes. When we women offer our experience as truth, as human truth, all the maps change. There are new mountains."

A cognitive linguist focused on political change, George Lakoff studies how we respond to stories and how our behavior is influenced by the narratives and metaphors we use. His research strongly suggests that we humans are hard-wired for story. That means that once we've heard a story and our hearts and minds have wrapped around it, no amount of facts to the contrary will get us to let go of that story. We environmentalists and social justice activists often assume that if we present the facts we can change people's minds, but it's become clear that the facts are not nearly as sticky or convincing as stories are. Only a more compelling story can alter people's prevailing narrative.

The author N. Scott Momaday famously said: "We live in a house made of stories." Stories are the seed forms of culture we carry around within us. Internalized, they define how expansively or tightly we offer the gift of our lives to the world. We decide how far we can go, how large a stand we're willing to make, or what risks we're willing to take, based upon the stories we tell ourselves.

Sometimes these stories that help define us stem from our family, culture and social conditioning, and we carry them unwittingly, unaware of how they shape our lives, so it is crucial that we do the work of unpacking and making conscious the stories we tell ourselves.

About 10 years ago, I began unearthing my own hidden stories, and discovered that I thought of myself as *The woman behind the man* (and, as you may have heard: *behind every great man is a woman, rolling her eyes*). It was shocking to realize how self-limiting my inner narrative was. I was horrified to discover that this story or belief had unconsciously embedded itself within me. I asked other colleagues whether any of them — including my husband and partner — saw me that way. They did not. Once I understood that it was only my own story and not reflected by others around me, I understood that I held the keys to my own liberation. This insight expanded my definition of leadership, and an awareness of the centrality of stories has informed and guided my path ever since.

Sometimes stories can help us to reconnect with emotions that have been banished or anesthetized. Given the scope of the losses we face, with species extinctions happening at an unimaginable rate, anger, loss, powerlessness and grief are totally appropriate responses. Culturally, however, we have no rituals, no safe places to express those anymore. Stories can reopen us, allowing us to feel our emotions in a healthy way so that we can risk casting aside our numbness to respond to these crises from an awakened and alive place. Those kinds of stories are needed to heal our relations with our selves, each other and this endangered, sacred Earth that is our home. We tend to be far more adept at resisting what we don't want than articulating a future story of what we yearn for with all our hearts. To paraphrase Yogi Berra: "If we're not careful, we're going to end up where we're heading."

I believe the need for a clear vision of where we want to go is essential to help us connect with and inspire a broad range of people and to help us develop the stamina and persistence we will need in the years ahead. Much of Bioneers' emphasis over the years has been to inspire people to act on behalf of a future they want, to understand how interdependent all the issues confronting us are, and to highlight those stories that can motivate us to help build the sort of movement of movements we now need to save our species from its own worst impulses. It's vital that we tell stories of a future that's believable, emotionally accessible, sensually connectable, and that we passionately want. I agree with Charles Eisenstein that we're in a time "between stories." There's a story of fear, separation and scarcity, based upon domination, ranking and greed. It's got a long and bloody history, and we've all had lots of practice adapting to it.

The emergent story is one of solidarity, of relatedness, of empathy, giving and sharing. It includes meaningful rituals to mark changes and to form new relationships and life passages, respect and appreciation for diversity and for the sacredness of all life, and operates on principles of inclusion and mutuality. This new culture will simultaneously draw from the best of humanity's ancient wisdom and the most positive emergent new ideas. It's a story of the relationship economy, not one based upon exploitation and transactions. This story has at its foundation the shifting of focus and priority in our societies from counting things to mapping connectedness. It's the story of a security that's based upon love, rather than material acquisition.

We've learned that it's neither fear nor threat that allows us to change people's minds or behavior, it's having a more enticing story — a narrative that speaks to our hearts, that describes a future we would all wish to live in, one that we all want to be invited into. Oh, I want to live in that story. Yes, I want to contribute to that future, that vision that someone just so beautifully evoked in her poetry or song. That's the world I'm motivated to give my time, resources and love to co-creating.

Stories are also crucial to mending the pigeonholing, the false separations that our society tends to reinforce. They can enhance our empathy, our capacity to imagine walking in another's shoes. Most of us yearn for intimacy and deep relationship. Really listening to others' stories and sharing some of our own are among the most effective pathways to transforming our cultures and growing deep connections. They work on us through identification with the storyteller, connecting us with those we might not normally see or hear. They are medicine for our false isolation, a way to forge connection and community and help shift our course.

Jensine Larson's remarkable global media project, World Pulse, which connects women from around the world to share their stories and create networks of mutual support, is an example of just the sort of story-based initiative we need. Fortunately, World Pulse is not alone. In the last few decades whole new bodies of story-based practices, some based in ancient Indigenous ways, some emerging from newly integrated understandings of neuroscience and psychology, have emerged. The practice of "Council," of which there are many variants, and a slew of hosting and convening approaches and methods that use storytelling as a cornerstone of their methodology, is spreading far and wide.

We're all involved in midwifing a new world into being, as the old world is crumbling around us. How do we engage with the tremendous uncertainty of the current human predicament? Joanna Macy uses an especially powerful storytelling-based exercise to teach us how to shift our relationship to time. This is an exercise that comes from her *Work that Reconnects*: Imagine that time travel is possible and that you're about to be visited by someone from seven generations in the future. A young person is coming back in time to interview you because you were alive in this pivotal moment. Take a moment to imagine and notice what you anticipate the tone of that interview might be, and let your body feel it. Notice any sensations that come up in your body, your heart, your mind or your spirit. Joanna suggests that this young person is coming back from the future because you are a hero or a *shero* to them. They are coming back so excited to ask you how you knew what to do. They ask you: "How did you navigate this extraordinary moment when everything about human civilization had to change? What can you teach me about how you gave yourself to this immense and essential transformation?" Again, notice any changes in your body, heart, mind, and spirit, and then, very gently, when you're ready, bring your attention back to the present moment.

Did you assume initially that somebody coming back from the future would be mad, or angry? I sure did. I was pretty convinced that would be their stance. When I heard Joanna frame it that *I was* the hero, *that I was here, that I helped make the change*, I thought, wow, look at that invisible bias that I carry! It's a story that anticipates and assumes — based in part on experience — that we good guys are losing. We have lots of reasons to have adopted that insidious belief: just turn on the nightly news, it gets reinforced all the time. But this is why it's so radical and so important to monitor and question our inner stories. We can support each other in knowing that the outcome being predicted in the media spin is not the final word. Our attitude towards what happens is key, and if we can show up for a positive outcome in a wholehearted and believable way, we can engage others to join us. As Gandhi said, "Social change occurs when deeply felt private experiences are given public legitimacy."

THE POWER OF STORY

EVE ENSLER

N o one illustrates the power of storytelling more profoundly than
Eve Ensler, whose lifework has brought home truths about the
foundational violence of our society: against women, and against the
Earth herself. Her art has revealed the centrality of our archetypally
wounded human relationship to matter, to our mother the Earth, and
to our selves. Sharing stories of women's relationships to their bodies,
she has inspired and mobilized millions while giving permission to
whole generations of women to heal, connect, and bear witness to
each other's transformations.

Twenty-something years ago, Eve Ensler did something
revolutionary: she began interviewing women of all ages, classes and
backgrounds to learn about how women related to their vaginas.
Though she initially anticipated writing a play based upon their stories,
neither she nor anyone else could have imagined the extraordinary
impact that play would have.

She soon discovered that she'd unearthed "the most reviled word
in the English language," and set about healing our vagina-phobic culture
through theater. Her award-winning play, *The Vagina Monologues*, provided
a startling window into the conflicted complexity of women's relationship
to their bodies, their sexuality and their very selves. While performing the
play throughout the world, Eve found lines of women backstage nightly,

waiting to tell her their stories of rape, incest, domestic battery and genital mutilation. They desperately needed to have their stories heard.

In 1998 a group of women in New York joined Eve to found V-Day, a movement that has raised over $50 million for grassroots groups around the world working to end violence against women. *The Vagina Monologues* has now been translated into 45 languages and performed in over 120 countries. It has become an unparalleled vehicle to help raise awareness and funds to end violence against women and transform this societal pattern the world over.

When Eve was diagnosed with cancer and learned it had spread to many organs in her body, she went through an arduous and lengthy healing process. Through her hospital window, she drew strength from a tree she could see from her bed. She realized that growing up in a city, she'd never really related to the healing power and mystery of the natural world. As she healed, she fell in love with nature, which she then wrote about in her cancer memoir, *In the Body of the World*. Through her writing and activism she never stops transmuting her own trauma and healing into medicine for others as she pursues her dream of a nonviolent world based on cooperation, dialogue and care.

Art that has demonstrated a real and significant impact on global societies within a short period of time is rare. One could make a case that *The Vagina Monologues* might just be the set of stories that has had the most dramatic, continuing, ongoing positive social impact in history. It has become more of a tidal wave, an unparalleled cultural phenomenon, rather than simply a play. It has captured the imaginations of and given voice to girls and women around the world, and it's been performed in places where women risk their lives to participate. Eve did not just create an incredibly successful, "viral," self-replicating art form to further women's human rights, already an extraordinary achievement. She has since co-created a movement and on-the-ground institutions to support women around the world in healing from violence, with funding and concrete assistance.

In response to a fact-finding mission to the Congo, V-day launched a campaign in partnership with UNICEF and thousands of activists on the ground to raise awareness about the epidemic level of gender violence in that nation. Together, they seeded and helped fund the creation of the City of Joy in Bukavu, where women survivors of sexual violence can go to live and be healed.

Eve takes a lot of heat for being idealistic in aiming to end violence against women. It takes a particular kind of courage to take such a powerful stand, regardless of the odds. She has worked tirelessly to create powerful political and artistic antidotes to brutality against women and girls, and she is continuously pushing the envelope, launching new initiatives to further that goal.

Her most recent project, One Billion Rising, continues that legacy but takes it in a new direction, using dance and celebration in events around the globe. She describes her vision this way: "Every February, we will rise — in hundreds of countries across the world — to show our local communities and the world what one billion looks like and shine a light on the rampant impunity and injustice that survivors most often face. We rise through dance to express joy and community and celebrate the fact that we have not been defeated by this violence. We rise to show we are determined to create a new kind of consciousness — one where violence will be resisted until it is unthinkable."

A couple of years ago, at a Bioneers conference, Eve offered a performance piece that had caught hold of her imagination in the weeks just before. Though she'd planned to give a different talk, she wrote to me to ask "is it ok if I do this thing that's coming through

now, that's quite radical?" On stage, she performed "Eve's Revolution,"
a truly inspired (and extremely funny) reimagining of what had actually
happened between Adam and Eve. She recast that archetypal, ancient
and deeply rooted narrative, a story that has so heavily contributed to the
subjugation of women, and transformed it into a tale of feminine wisdom
and empowerment. It may have been the most brilliant and subversive
form of artistic creation I have ever witnessed, one that revealed the
awesome power of storytelling to reimagine and remake the world.

I invite you all to practice storytelling every chance you get. Here are
a few practical tips that I've gleaned from Eve and some of my other mentors:

- Include details that enliven your listeners' senses, that
  speak to their embodied realities.
- Use the simplest possible language and be specific.
- Encourage your imagination to roam freely, to envision
  and share far-reaching tales of the future/the changes
  you want to see.
- Resist telling people what they should think, feel or
  do. Instead, model what you're offering through your
  own transformative experience. This invites peoples's
  imaginations to engage more deeply.
- Don't be afraid to share your emotional truth and
  reveal your vulnerability.
- Don't inflate your own importance: humility and
  humor are critical elements of any good story.
- Speak personally and subjectively; own your own
  experience. This is the best way to help open pathways
  for others to honor and respect their own experiences.

I leave you with a metaphor and prayer I learned from Janine Benyus, the godmother of the emerging field of biomimicry: *May we all learn to carry stories like birds carry seeds in their feathers, to help seed the vision of a new world. Whenever an ecosystem has been traumatized or decimated, it can be brought back to life by the seeds that birds carry on their feathers. In the course of their living, flying and eating, they drop those seeds in seemingly random places, to reignite fertility and diversity, as well as hope, regeneration and life.*

CELEBRATING WOMEN'S WAYS

I find myself appreciating women —
and valuing what we bring to the world —
in this writhing, frightening change-time, more every day.

And I so deeply admire men who are
learning from women's ways,
becoming better listeners, rotating leadership,
and staying connected to others —
even while you stay true to your own purposes.
Remembering the value of beauty,
relatedness, flexibility, pausing and reflection.

I am oddly reassured by the ancient prophesies
that predicted this would be a time
for the return of the Feminine —
a time for re-balancing the world.

Perhaps I seek reassurance from our ancestors,
for what I already know, deep in my bones,
is true and needed and right.

I'm discovering aspects of myself as a woman

that I'd largely abandoned,
ones that are larger than I've allowed myself to be,
parts that are fierce, fiery and feisty,
also playful, sure-footed and wise.

Before, I imagined them too dangerous to reveal.
Now, I feel called to bring all of me to bear —
from the place of my own commitment,
from the place of my deep love for people and nature and culture.
My fear pales in comparison with what's at stake.

I remember that we teach young women
to be good by following the rules,
coloring inside the lines, and not making waves.
We're taught to keep our heads low — to avoid conflict.
To be good at caring for others, and knowing what they need —
often well ahead of knowing our own needs, ourselves.

But we expect young men to rebel.
To find their own identity,
they're encouraged to defy the norms,
to stand firm in their own convictions,
and to step out on their own.
Boys are applauded for taking risks,
and for bragging, or boasting
about their achievements.

Girls are told to demure and be quiet.
Admonished not to show off,

"not to be so full of yourself."
(Who are we supposed to be full of,
        we might wonder, if not ourselves?)

Many of us are learning, now,
to turn that caring and nurturing inward as well,
and to toss out some of our good-girl conditioning,
to step out and fulfill our purposes
in creative, risky and authentic ways.

How encouraging to find women emerging everywhere,
stepping out of our safety zones,
mirroring and complementing each other's strength and vulnerability —
which is the "power through," not "power over" that is the essence
of power being redefined and reclaimed
        by women all over.

What do I love most about women?
(As reminders for us all
about women's magnificence
in this transitional time.)

When women interact intimately,
there's a lot more going on than an exchange of ideas.
We absorb each other's textures, scents, and colors.
We inhale each other's bearing,
intuiting undercurrents of childhood,
gleaning molecules of emotion —
our bodies trade a hundred unspoken cues.

As women enter deeper relational waters,
our enthusiasms become infectious,
our beginnings and endings blur, seamlessly.
We enjoy the rhythms we form with each other,
concepts coinciding as our passions swirl.

We not only braid our thoughts, ideas and feelings together,
we let our memories mingle with our intuitions and our dreams.
I love how often women remember how much we don't know —
and that our intuition or silence, dreams or deep listening
often bring whatever is most needed.

At our best, we weave our worlds together,
contrasting combinations of disparate realities.
Creating a multicolored canvas thick with texture and pigment.

Changing our moods and minds as often as the winds —
but rarely our hearts, our truest compasses.

As women, our bodies and the moon instruct us
to recognize the cyclical nature of change.

We understand innately that the destruction and death
all around us
        also mean that a birth is imminent.

Each of us, men and women alike,
are being asked to assist in this labor.
To deliver the profound, fierce, single-focused commitment to life

that accompanies any successful birth.

The midwives know that
     it's just when the labor is becoming most
          scary, bloody and intense,
just when the mother feels she cannot
     bear the pain any further —
that is when you know that
     the baby is about to be born.

As women, we attentively attune to our bodies,
relishing the pulses of deep knowing that come
from our bellies.

Together, we knit dimensional patterns of our laughter,
anger, sadness, and the holy water of our tears.

We yearn to mend the tattered fragments,
to turn our anger into compassionate action.
To integrate the painful, frightening,
enraged hot beauty and the flows of
 laughter, unity and celebration into
     dancing a new world into being.

PART III

Toward Wholeness

GENDER EQUITY AND RACIAL JUSTICE

VALUING RELATIONSHIP & TRADITION

Towards a Future That Works for All

As seasonal cycles become wobblier, migrations increasingly uncertain and food harvests ever more unpredictable, wars rage, hurricanes land and millions flee their homes. This past year police violence against African Americans became so widely visible it reached a tipping point. Political vitriol has been flashing hotter and meaner, reigniting misogyny, fear and hatred in millions. In many places the sweet waters of Mother Earth have become too toxic to drink, and Indigenous protectors gathered this year from all directions to try and stop the plunder for the sake of future generations and all life on Earth.

I've been listening for guidance. Life has been teaching me to look for patterns to help me understand what's needed to shift our culture, to reorient toward what's sacred and whole.

The first way I learned taught me to balance my body, heart, mind and spirit. Using those filters helped me to witness myself. It required listening to what my body knew, and heeding my emotions, dreams and intuition, as well as the reasoning of my mind.

Helping knit women together in song and dance, story and ritual — to share our vulnerabilities in webs of relational caring and empathic connection — can fling open the possibilities of healing, collaboration and aligned sisterhood.

Being in ceremony, practicing ritual and story with open hearts, is what's made those relationships across differences possible. I now believe that these practices could yield the same results toward healing and forging connection among all caring people.

I've seen how recognizing the truths of our shared yet differing wounds can create pathways for our factionalized women's movements to grow into the larger web of resistance, voice and power that is needed to reclaim our democracy and shift our course.

Recently, I visited friends who live traditionally on the Penticton Indian reservation in the Okanagan region of British Columbia. I share these learnings humbly and cautiously, as I am aware of my "outsider" or "settler" reality, with no intent of misappropriating Native culture.

My only purposes are towards learning and healing, and honoring the immense value of Indigenous knowledge traditions to us all in this precarious time. I visited Penticton during their seasonal Salmon Ceremony, a time when I could experience their practices of nurturing their relationships with the land, their community, the river, the salmon and their traditions.

The Okanagan culture is designed around teachings called the Four Societies, or Enowkin'wixw. It is an ancient social technology that has taught them through generations how to relate in a balanced and respectful way to all the various parts of people, community and Mother Earth.

The idea of the Four Societies reminds us that it's necessary to respect, include and accommodate them all equally in our decision-making. As Jeannette Armstrong, culture bearer and educator from the Okanagan Syilx Nation, puts it: *Our tradition demands four things from us and they all have equal weight.*

The Four Societies are: tradition and vision, relationship and action.

The **tradition society** relates to what's worked before, to the land and the sacred. It corresponds to the elder within us.

The **vision society** focuses on what's ahead, on the future, on what creatively has yet to come. It is related to the energy of youth.

The **relationship society** is responsible for caring for any impacts or influences of a decision upon the people, and all beings. It is related to the feminine archetype.

The **action society** focuses on how to do things, on analysis, implementation, sequencing, tools and resources. It is related to the masculine part of our psyches.

People are trained by their elders to listen and speak for one of each of the four societies.

Any decision the people make *must* integrate all four perspectives with full equality. This approach from the Okanagan culture is an ancient, living blueprint for Justice, Equity and Inclusion.

Reflecting on the Four Societies, I see how often we've privileged vision and action over tradition and relationship. I see how our systems and structures have perpetuated a bias, a deeply-entrenched valuing of only two of the four. Vision and Action have systematically trumped Tradition and Relationship.

In scanning for patterns among Indigenous philosophies, I see how deeply tradition, land and relationship are valued. In the

Okanagan language, for instance, the word they use for their bodies contains the word for land within it. "We're not just part of the land," Jeannette writes, "the land IS us."

From Tiokasin Ghosthorse I learned that in the Lakota language, the word for soil means "who we used to be." Imagine remembering that relationship to Mother Earth each time we mention soil.

As Jeannette writes: "When we include the perspective of the land, and we include the perspective of relationships, people in the community actually change. The desire to secure material wealth and fear of not having 'things' to sustain you disappear. When you start realizing that people and community are there to sustain you, this gives the most secure feeling in the world."

I call that the relationship economy. When the 2008 economic crisis hit, I knew that the only real security lay in the web of relationships each of us has, cultivates and cares for.

Arriving at the Salmon Ceremony, we drove into a provincial park adjacent to the Okanagan river. The day sparkled with dappled sunlight, and the feast had just begun.

While most of the people there were from the traditional tribal community, others included international students and locals who were curious, or friends. Walking in, everyone was welcoming. Each person I met gazed into my eyes with warmth, curiosity and dignity. Everyone was served, a couple hundred of us, and the salmon was sweet and moist.

Afterward, the salmon's bones and entrails were returned ceremonially with blessings to the river. There was a purification ceremony. To traditional drumming and time-honored songs, at the river's edge a woman prayed as she cleansed each person in turn.

At an open mic, Okanagan cousins from Texas had just come from Standing Rock. They spoke with pride of the determination of the Protectors there, noting how many peoples from so many nations were gathering, and praising how their Lakota friends were welcoming everyone, regardless of their background or color.

Next came a give-away, where this community which has so little monetarily, and yet are so wealthy culturally, distributed gifts to everyone assembled. Four tarps were mounded high with goodies and one by one, with timeless patience and care, accompanied by traditional songs and the frolicking laughter of children, all were gifted.

Generosity and kindness, patience and gratitude filled the air. When I left, I felt suffused with thankfulness. I had the sense that I'd experienced something of the "preferred state" that Buckminster Fuller spoke about. That state of equilibrium and reciprocity where all is in right relationship.

Well, almost. The contrast between the beauty, richness and power of their cultural practices and the financial poverty and malnourishment of so many of their people pierced my heart. I wept much of the way home to the U.S., as the contrast was overwhelming, and I was overflowing with gratitude.

May we have the humility to listen for guidance from the land, from our ancestors, and from our bodies and hearts, minds and intuition.

May we then have the wisdom to hear it, and act upon it, even if it comes from the least expected places.

May we face this fractured young nation's history — built upon genocide and slavery, lies, broken promises and domination — and choose, for the sake of healing, to walk through the fear and traumas, tears and fires needed for healing, together.

May we find the collective vision, courage and will to decolonize our minds and hearts, reclaiming a balance of feminine & masculine, of tradition and vision, relationship and action in equal measure that will flow through each of us to all.

HEALING AT THE INTERSECTIONS
Environment and Social Justice Conjoin at Bioneers

Nina Simons' acceptance speech for the 2017 Goi Peace Award. Based in Tokyo, the Goi Peace Foundation established this annual award in 2000 to recognize individuals and organizations that have contributed to creating a peaceful and harmonious world as well as building a better future.

First, I wish to express my deepest gratitude to the Goi Peace Foundation, for honoring Kenny and me, and Bioneers, with this award. We accept this honor with humility, and on behalf of the large and extended community of those visionaries Kenny Ausubel — my partner, husband and co-founder — back in 1990, coined a term to describe: "Bioneers."

What we mean now by Bioneers is: scientific, political and social innovators, activists, cultural bridge-builders and leaders from many walks of life and fields of endeavor who are collaboratively contributing to the great global ecological and socio-cultural transformation now underway. It is an enormous validation that you here at the Goi Foundation, who have done so much to promote world peace, and are based halfway around the planet from the U.S., have heard of Bioneers and perceive value in our work. Thank you.

In accepting this honor, I wish to offer some reflections about what I think makes Bioneers a unique enterprise. On the physical plane, it's a relatively small nonprofit organization, but one that has developed into a key nexus for many diverse but intersecting social movements. It provides a forum annually that highlights some of the most inspiring and practical solutions to humanity's most pressing crises. We sometimes call it a "network of networks." In fact, it's a dynamic, ever-evolving living system whose goal is to help co-create, midwife and nurture a new world, the birth of a new civilization, one that's far more peaceful, equitable, healthy and resilient — goals that we, of course, share with you here.

We work toward a future that goes beyond the idea of sustainability as a goal. Merely sustaining ecosystems and communities — while much better than destroying them, as we currently so often do — we find to be too timid as an ultimate goal. We aim for not just a sustainable human footprint, but one that is regenerative for all of life. We seek the restoration of health and vitality to natural systems and to human communities by combining the best of ancient wisdom with the leading edge of contemporary "whole-systems" approaches.

At the heart of this notion is the idea that we humans need to be humble, to become students of nature's extraordinarily sophisticated design genius. We have to reorient our learning by observing how nature operates, and reinvent our civilizations by cooperating with her rather than by seeking to dominate her. This requires us to remember that there is wisdom all around us, including from our old-growth cultures, the Indigenous peoples of Earth. We see this collaborative vision as helping to strengthen life's capacity for healing and renewal through a respectful and loving partnership with life's mysterious, ancient and complex nature.

One of the foundations of our worldview is that, just as in the natural world in which the most diverse ecosystems are the most resilient and vital, the human enterprise also thrives best when it is characterized by high degrees of diversity. In our work, therefore, we have always sought to highlight a broad array of innovative approaches to solving problems, presented from diverse perspectives, disciplines, generations and cultures, including a very strong emphasis on honoring the wisdom of Indigenous "First Peoples" and of long-lived traditional ecological wisdom.

At a conference in 1994, the physicist, ecologist and activist Vandana Shiva from India offered some crucial distinctions between a "bioneer" and a pioneer. She warned that rapid scientific innovations intended to improve upon biology posed tremendous risks. Highly aggressive biologists and corporations seeking to profit from poorly conceived genetic manipulation look very much like the European pioneers, who thought that every land they conquered was an empty land. They believed that land had no people, or no people that they respected as full human beings, so they saw no need to respect any pre-existing rights.

Those we have called bioneers, on the other hand, recognize that every step we take is on a full Earth populated by a tremendous variety of species and many other people. The pioneer "empty land" ethic, Shiva noted, "leads to violence against species and to genocide. The colonizing pioneer's mind assumes there are no limits to be respected, no ecological limits, no ethical limits, no limits to greed or accumulation, no limits to inequality. No limits to the violence to be unleashed on other species and people." And no limits to seeking to reshape molecules in complex living systems that we don't understand.

"Whereas authentic bioneers," she said, "know that limits are the first law of nature, encoded in the ecological processes that make life possible. Limits of the nutrient cycle in soil, limits of the water cycle. The limits set by the intrinsic right of diverse species to exist set limits on our actions, if we genuinely respect other beings. Ethical limits are what make us human. To be sustainable, a society must live within those limits."

Shiva spoke of a Hindi term, *vasudhaiva kutumbakam*, that means "We are one-earth family," or the "democracy of life." She explained that "to bioneers, it means not just diverse human cultures, but all beings. The mountains and the rivers are beings too. We bioneers respect all the beings, large and small, without a hierarchy of superiority and inferiority, because everything has a part to play ecologically in the web of life, even if we do not fully understand how."

And being a bioneer also means recognizing that, just as the web of life is interconnected and interdependent, so too are all the issues we face.

Over time, the large annual conference we have produced for the past 28 years expanded to present a wider spectrum of interrelated issues and solutions. It became increasingly clear to me that there could no longer be any perceived separation between people and the "environment." We are a part of nature, not apart from it. We are not separate from the environment or from nature. Our bodies are made of the same materials, the same DNA as plants, fungi and animals. We are all connected, both biologically and spiritually. Since the Earth is a closed loop, the cup of tea you drink today may have once been Cleopatra's bathwater.

What we do to the Earth, we do to ourselves. When we harm ourselves and other people, we wound the Earth. Therefore, being a bioneer *must* include pursuing social justice and equity for all humans as well as protecting ecosystems.

For the first 10 years or so, I used the term "bioneer" to describe the people on stage, the presenters we invited to speak, leading figures who offered brilliant new approaches and practical models of ecological or social restoration. I was unconscious of my own internalized hierarchy, but all that changed when the late J.L. Chestnut spoke in 2001. He was a renowned attorney and legendary Civil Rights activist since the brutal struggles in the U.S. South of the 1950s, and he expanded my definition of a bioneer into something larger.

He was telling the story of winning the largest class action lawsuit in the history of America — against the U.S. Government for institutional racism against Black farmers in the southeastern U.S. It was a powerful talk, and he did something I'd never heard before. He began to use the word *bioneer* to address everyone in the room.

He noted that the progress that's being made, slowly but surely, to bring our country toward racial and social justice and true democracy was due in part to the efforts of "You bioneers, dedicated progressive people like you." He went on to say, "I raise these concerns to you because fighting on behalf of women, on behalf of minority people of color, fighting on behalf of the environment and the planet are all one big battle. We bioneers know that violence, greed, racism, unchecked materialism, and abuse of this planet and the nature in and on it is its own form of terrorism, and will eventually destroy us if we don't first put an end to it."

It was a revelatory moment for me. Suddenly, that word didn't just describe the visionary innovators on stage, but applied to us all. Not only the speakers, but every man, woman and child present, or

hearing Bioneers podcasts or radio, or seeing our videos, or anyone
working toward healing our relationship with Earth in thousands of
different ways.

We each had a role to play. We were all *bioneers*, if we chose to
be. All our contributions, all our collective creativity and imagination
were needed to help reinvent this world.

As J.L. Chestnut said, the way our cultures have treated women,
people of color, Indigenous people, immigrants and the Earth are
all just different octaves of the same legacy. We all, regardless of our
differences, bear the scars of a culture that's founded on conquest,
exploitation and oppression. This tendency we have shown over time,
to invest in the false myths of superiority or separation, seems to be at
the root of our common challenges. With patterns so entrenched, so
pervasive and so overwhelming, how can we shift our course?

I began to see that we're all, in varying ways, responding to often
unconscious influences and implicit biases from a legacy of disrespect
and violence that manifests on all levels of society — from the personal,
emotional and physical, to the economic, political and environmental.

Thankfully, we also know the power of community and
connection, and we are gifted with a capacity for self-reflection and
choice. Each time we opt to relate caringly, choosing to meet others on
common ground instead of reinforcing separation with those whose
views may differ, we begin to help heal and restore our social landscape.
Each time we renew ourselves in nature, sensing with our full bodies,
hearts and intuitions the repair and guidance she so abundantly offers,
we help the healing happen.

During the years since, Bioneers has evolved greatly, prompted
in part by this understanding.

We've sought to design for a whole-systems approach to how people learn. Since people process information in different ways — integrating audio, visual and kinesthetic information with varying priorities — we've designed sessions that speak to those multiple ways of perceiving. Appreciating that diversity includes speaking to introverts and extroverts, creative and analytical thinkers, people of all ages and ethnicities and disciplines and also of all classes, orientations and abilities, we strive to be as inclusive and accessible as possible. We hope to meet people where they are, and reach peoples's hearts through their rational minds and sensing bodies, as well as their intuition and values.

We are also committed to not shying away from the difficult conversations, the challenging, complex issues, in order to deepen our own understanding and learning.

We hope to educate, inspire and ignite engaged action, while identifying and illuminating the most promising solutions and strategies. By juxtaposing seemingly disparate issues and mingling them with arts and ceremony, we help reveal how all issues are part of one dynamic, interrelated living system, which embeds us within the context of the living world.

We all need each other to make the large-scale changes we face. Relationships of authentic cooperation, collaboration and community will become absolutely critical in the years ahead, because we are facing immense challenges. Bridging our differences respectfully will determine whether or not we succeed at shifting human civilization from our current ecocidal trajectory.

In the past several years, I have realized that for me to be able to help create effective change "*out there*" in the world, I have to also work on seeing — and then changing — myself. There have been many ways in which I have internalized the unresolved wounds, blind spots and biases of our U.S. culture, from gender bias to racial injustice. I am trying hard to reconcile them, to make peace within myself.

As I've searched for insights to help me in this quest, I've come to feel that, while racial divides still roil and rupture our societies — and I can't imagine experiencing the discrimination and micro-aggressions so many minority people experience each day — the biases that privilege the masculine over the feminine create at least as great an unconscious barrier to equity and peace among people as faith, race or cultural differences. In recent years, studies have shown gender to be the bias most deeply embedded in the human psyche globally.

Like most women, I've experienced thousands of moments of feeling diminished, threatened or intimidated because of my gender. Inwardly, I also see ways I've unconsciously acquired some learned beliefs about women and limited my own options and pathways as a result.

But I realize that gender and race are only two of the many ways we diminish each other and ourselves. Nearly all of us have experienced feeling slighted or disrespected somewhere, whether for our ethnicity, age, size, sexual preference, ability, class or appearance. While I am inspired to see that much progress has occurred in some of these areas, we have far more work to do to heal the wounds that separate us.

I believe that investing in the leadership of women — and restoring the "feminine" to a place of equilibrium with the "masculine" throughout all of our lived experience as individuals, as well as in our institutions and culture — are essential to the global transformation that we, as a species, are being called to make, in order to shift our course to a life-affirming future on Earth.

Around the globe, we see clearly that wherever the rights, opportunities and safety of women improve, benefits result for all areas of society. As women's leadership and gender equity increase, so too do economic prosperity, public health, education, peace and the security of nations. As women's education and reproductive rights improve globally, they will also have significant effects in curbing population growth, drawing down carbon and slowing climate change.

Since we've inherited some skewed stereotypes about what the masculine and feminine really mean, I suggest we seek to identify and reclaim healthy identities that can include and embrace a full array of our human capacities, regardless of what our physical gender identity might be.

We need the full generative capacity of the active principle, informed by the best listening and guidance of the receptive within us all, to succeed together at collectively midwifing a peaceful, regenerative and just world, to be born out of this turbulence.

Since we all contain masculine and feminine within us, this is ultimately about restoring our human wholeness. About practicing listening and not-knowing, more often than asserting that we know the answers. About evolving from power over to power with and power to co-create change. It's about trusting that leadership is often better shared, and that win-win solutions frequently exist, if we seek them out patiently, practicing mutual respect, patience and trust.

As Indigenous peoples of the Amazon say, "the bird of humanity has been trying to fly for far too long with only one wing."

May we have the humility to listen for guidance from the land, from our ancestors, and from our bodies and hearts, as well as our minds, dreams and intuition. May we have the wisdom to hear it, and act upon it, even if it comes from the least expected or most surprising places.

May we find the collective vision, courage and will to decolonize our minds and hearts, reclaiming a balance of feminine & masculine, of receptive and active, of yin and yang in equal measure that flow through us each and all.

May our partnership with the land, our mother Earth, Gaia, and the sweet and salty waters that flow in her veins, the winds and clouds that caress and bathe her, and the fires that cleanse and restore her vitality, and our kinship with all the creatures large and small who share this sacred home become our devotional, long-term relationship practice.

May this lead us collectively toward a world that's re-infused with a sense of the sacred, where the future children of all species live and flourish in peace, and where restorative justice, health and regeneration thrive.

Awomen. Amen. May it be so. Thank you.

ESCAPING THE TILTED ROOM

H as anyone among us not felt powerless, experienced being the dissenting or minority voice, or felt unfairly judged, devalued or dismissed for being different?

We have all experienced a culture that elevates some while denigrating others. As a young woman right out of college, for some years I believed the feminist movement had accomplished its goals, and that I was stepping onto a level playing field. That same naïveté, mixed with idealism and some cultural blindness, also had me imagining that the Civil Rights Movement had largely ended racial bias and injustice in this country.

It wasn't until much later — after years of being the only woman in business settings, of negotiating biased gender dynamics personally, professionally and politically, that I began to realize how much gender roles and related power dynamics were impacting my experience — and how painful and damaging those impacts were.

It wasn't until several years after that, when I began peeling back the layers of my own defensiveness and denial, that I began to learn how racialized our society still is, and to discover my own personal and cultural complicity in it. Gender and race are only two of the ways we rank and compete with each other — benefiting some, and harming others. In this society, we also create hierarchies based on age, sexual orientation, body shape, class, education and abilities, to name just a few.

As I work to integrate and distill what I've been learning, an especially useful metaphor for me is the "Tilted Room." I found it in Melissa Harris-Perry's book *Sister Citizen*, about the stereotypes that Black women in America encounter as they work to establish a unique identity, and achieve agency and recognition. She describes a cognitive psychology experiment in which people were placed in a crooked chair within a crooked room, and asked to align themselves vertically. Researchers were surprised that — even in a room tilted as much as 35° — some people reported that they were perfectly straight, simply because they were in alignment with their surroundings. Only a few managed to find uprightness.

As Harris-Perry notes, "It can be hard to stand up straight in a crooked room." We're all products of a culture that's filled with tilted rooms, spaces designed to get us to relate in ways that defy the natural instincts of our bodies, hearts and souls. Though the room may be tipped according to differing sets of biases, it's rarely level. Some benefit from a headwind, while many face persistent and systematized obstacles.

Our dysfunctional families, educational institutions, media, cities, food and health care, economic and political systems create and reinforce striated structures of race, class, gender and other "isms" that keep us apart. Since these biases aren't conducive to symbiosis, and we all contain both victim and perpetrator within us, we become stuck in win/lose, dualistic and polarizing dynamics. The systems that tilted rooms represent, and those biased perceptions and the policies and social structures they inform, keep us divided — preventing collaboration, coalition and movement-building.

And, though it may seem otherwise, they damage the ones who benefit from the tilt as much as those who are disadvantaged by it. They hurt us all.

At a Cultivating Women's Leadership intensive, the women of color requested a time to caucus, where they could visit together apart from the white women. (I'll never forget this, as the sensory image is forever imprinted in my memory.) Across the lawn, the women of color and Indigenous women gathered on a porch. Like birds with showy plumage, they were a feast of vibrant color. With long dresses, scarves, painted toenails and hair done in ribbons, their visual expression was glorious and brilliant. Sound-wise too, they were expressive, as gales of laughter, a musicality in their voices and an occasional shout carried across the space between us.

Among the white women's group, everyone was wearing white and khaki. Their faces were glum, and their expressions sad, guilty and depressed. They couldn't understand why such a division might be needed, and why it had been initiated. As they hesitantly voiced their chagrin at feeling the separation, I noted how much the dimming of our light, the quieting of our voices, as white women, might be a cost of our unearned privilege.

How do we escape the tilted room? It is no small feat. It requires practice to disengage from those prevalent, insidious beliefs within us that help keep it in place. It requires a willingness to learn, humility about what we don't see or know, and a choice to shift our perception and understanding.

It asks that we reorient ourselves toward reaching across these divisions of gender, race and class — *and be willing to risk and to fail, for the sake of learning.* It means strengthening that intrinsic relational intelligence that comes from our body's wisdom, our heart's guidance and our moral compass.

Being white, or male, or heterosexual, or middle class, or highly educated, or rich or successful makes it particularly difficult to recognize that a tilt exists. But if you're on the losing end of the tilt, it's hard to ever forget, or not feel, the injustice of it, every hour of the day. One friend, a leader of mixed ethnicity, told me she felt as if she is continually climbing uphill on her knees, with broken glass strewn across her path — while white folks have running shoes, a clear walkway, and the wind at their backs.

Hearing the truth of others' realities, and sensing how painful they've been, I have realized that I previously grappled with injustice principally through my rational analysis and intellect — and from a distance that my privilege afforded me. Now, trying to listen at the deepest level, while loving and respecting the beauty, dignity and power I see in others' lived truths, has wrought a deeper change in me.

To overcome the tilted room, to heal ourselves from the habit of ranking, will require amplifying our listening to our hearts, intuitions and bodies. Our minds as primary navigator tend to perpetuate patterns, and are treacherously good at inventing stories to rationalize behavior that seems "normal," because it's habituated. It's only by strengthening those ways of knowing and choosing to keep our hearts open, receptive to others' pain, and feeling, that we can shift these insidious patterns and break free of the chronic tilt.

Many women across the nation and the world experienced it on the historic day of the January 2017 Women's March. It was transformative to see the kindness, creativity and care that were exhibited that day, as well as to sense the joy of feeling aligned with others who are different, focusing on connection and commonality of purpose. No one was arrested. All were respectful. It gave us all a palpable sense of what's possible, together.

It also revealed the shadow side of women's leadership. During the weeks and months that followed, I read on social media rants by sub-groups who felt they'd been snubbed, disrespectfully treated and were angered at the ignorance of many of the newcomers there. Generations of wounding revealed deep rifts among diverse women, where little empathy or understanding has been encouraged or taught. Frustration emerged from women of color, demanding rightfully that white women take responsibility for educating themselves. White women's feelings were hurt, and some of them turned away. Of course, the media featured and exaggerated these rifts.

As I practice getting better at appreciating these gifts (of feeling, intuition and embodied awareness), I recognize and encourage them more, both in myself and others. This is helping to free me from tilted rooms, strengthening my resolve, and increasing my toolkit toward co-creating the beloved community which is my heart's deepest yearning.

Thankfully, we can cultivate relationship intelligence by choosing it.

One specific practice that I've discovered is that my body's reactions — when I think someone might have said something racially or otherwise offensive to another — are far more reliable than my mind. As my mother taught me, my body never lies. If I pay close attention, I notice that my stomach lurches when I hear something that could be perceived as harmful, though it likely was not intended to be. If I am paying adequate attention to notice this in myself, then I can say, *"My stomach just let me know that what you just said might have been hurtful or felt off to another in the room. Is that true?"* In that way, I can take responsibility for stopping the conversation, creating a pause so that if a harm was felt, it can be unpacked and learned from. By responding to my body's signals, I don't need to accuse anyone, or presuppose intent, but can simply notice a disturbance in the field.

Another story: I became friends with a young woman of mixed Lakota descent who participated in another CWL intensive. She was a young mother, a businesswoman, community organizer and a cancer survivor who had created innovative opportunities to help women from her nation to come together for healing. I was deeply impressed by her courage and creativity, found her wise well beyond her years, and admired her greatly.

Months after the retreat, I learned she was going through a difficult time, though I knew nothing of the details. I called her to offer my support and express my concern on her behalf. She told me that she'd recently learned that her two nieces — aged 8 and 12 — had been raped. Sobbing uncontrollably, she told me their names, and about what loving, innocent and tender young girls they'd been. She explained that the perpetrator lived within their family house, and that there were no counseling resources available to them. The girls were not willing to report the abuse, or leave their home. I listened to her express her pain, frustration and grief for over an hour. When I hung up the phone, I felt shattered.

I had known about rates of rape and sexual abuse of women in Indian Country, but I had known about them from afar. I had read articles and seen news reports on the systemic challenges of jurisdiction on reservations, on the increased incidence of rape and sex trafficking in oil and gas drilling camps and on reservation lands, and had felt an affronted indignation at the failures of our systems to protect Indigenous women and girls. Hearing this beloved friend wail her grief and frustration with the names and descriptions of her young kin brought the truth of that epidemic home to my heart, in a way I had not known before.

TRAUMA, RUPTURE AND REPAIR

O ne of the things that unites us deeply, as people, is that at some point, to become fully integrated, we all have to actually walk through the flames of the traumas that we and/or our ancestors have experienced. This is part of the shadow work we must address, the unconscious painful stuff we've put aside that must be walked through in order to heal and transcend those wounds, so that they don't continue to recycle in our lives.

Trauma lives in our bodies in insidious ways that are hard to ferret out because we've got so many layers of conditioning and adaptation on top of it, attempting to banish or brush it under the rug of our lived awareness. It often feels to me like peeling back layers of an onion skin in order to get at our core selves.

I am reminded what Canadian author and physician Gabor Maté says about addressing trauma: that it's not really about the event itself that happened, but about how that event stimulated a separation from self that must be addressed.

I hear a deep call to address some of the underlying wounds that we are carrying as individuals, as a society and through diverse cultural lineages today, to be able to move wholeheartedly towards co-creating the future we want and need. Over many years now of working with diverse women, there are some similarities in terms of intergenerational wounding that I believe all women carry as a result of the burning times. Whether we were the watchers, or the children or the ones who were burned, those ancestral memories are alive in us, as they occurred over the span of seven generations, in countries throughout Europe. Whether our ancestors were from Africa, Europe or Asia or from Native America, I believe we each have our own versions of those stories of oppression, conquest and persecution, and carry them in our bones or genetic memory.

There is certainly a great deal of intergenerational trauma among many of our brothers and sisters who are people of color. As there was also among my Jewish ancestors, who were chased out of every land they ever called home, often violently. In many ways, these United States, with all of our myths of democracy, is built on a core of rot, and I've been increasingly feeling called to stand in solidarity with Indigenous people and all of those who are standing on behalf of the sacredness of life in all its forms, and for justice.

Thanks to the brilliant words and voices of Ta-Nehisi Coates and Michelle Alexander, perceiving the New Jim Crow, and in solidarity with my many beloved friends who share African American descent, I now feel called to stand with Black Lives Matter and the Movement for Black Lives. I've had to recognize that the U.S. Capitol and the White House were built by slaves, and to acknowledge the serial efforts at genocide that Indigenous people have suffered as well the appalling history of land theft, forced relocation and broken promises. I've had to accept what Ta-Nehisi Coates calls the "bloody heirloom" of this nation: the intentional and structurally reinforced myth of white supremacy.

Although there are similarities across our cultures, of course all of our stories are very different. But I think we're living at a time where the experience of trauma is widely available and it's important for us as women who want to bring our best selves to this moment, to be able to look it squarely in the face and see how we can bring ourselves to being effective agents of healing.

Now the question is: How do we begin to repair our relations with the Earth and the dysfunctional social systems that we live with? It's a question of relationship, because we live in a world where so many of our relationships have been ruptured.

My beloved mentor Dawna Markova taught me that "Relationships are a function of rupture and repair." I invite you to consider this premise, whether you're thinking about your family or your loved one or your spouse or your kids. We all have fights and face conflicts; we all have ruptures — that's what happens in relationships in the inevitable process of negotiating between two lived realities. It's whether and how you choose to turn towards repair that confers strength and resilience to our relationships.

I believe we have massive repair work ahead of us, and it needs to begin in the most intimate place first, with our selves. We have to repair our relationship with ourselves, with the Earth, and also with our families, our friends, our neighbors. But as we work on ourselves, in order to stand against the serial assaults we face, we must stand together with those who may not look, act or seem like us. But as the mystics teach through the ages, and traditional cultures have always noted, they are us. As my friend Ilarion Merculieff, a traditional wisdom keeper from the Unangan people, likes to remind me: in his village, when greeting another, it's customary to say, "Hello, my other self."

This commitment means sitting in discomfort sometimes, not knowing who's right, or whether or how to repair, and not running away. That discomfort has often come up for me in addressing issues, moments or comments about racial justice issues and white privilege.

I find that staying present while I'm uncertain and uncomfortable is a muscle I can strengthen through practice. It's also helpful in colleague, family or partner relationships. If we are willing to give focus, time and love to practicing this, along with real commitment, we can evolve through a lot of messy growing pains to be able to work together in a new and regenerative way.

An incident that pierced the shell of my privilege occurred during one of the Cultivating Women's Leadership workshops that I co-facilitated with cofounder Toby Herzlich in a rural retreat site in Northern New Mexico. Our time together included a collective dive into the pain of racial wounding. We heard about the Chinese grandmother whose bound feet hurt so much she had to be carried, the great uncle who had been lynched in the South, the Peruvian Indigenous grandmother who had been forced to leave her ancestral lands, the woman of mixed ancestry who had grown up ashamed and targeted because she was the darkest of her siblings. A white woman spoke of her slave-owner lineage, and acknowledged the shame and guilt she feels, alongside of her privilege. We listened to each other's stories deeply, and held each other tenderly. We noted how darkness is widely demonized. We named positive associations for Black and darkness, to reclaim their value.

We collaborated to create and enact an embodied healing ritual. Each of us made a symbolic piece from nature artifacts that spoke to us, often twigs, branches and weeds, and tied messages to it with colored yarn, that captured the hurts and beliefs we sought to shed. With help from the cleansing spirit of fire, a drum to connect our heartbeats, and naming the aspects within ourselves that we sought to release, one by one we burned the beautiful pieces of ceremonial art we'd made. We basked in the sense of liberation and alliance we felt in witnessing each other's work.

On the last night, Toby and I were awakened at 3 a.m. One of the women was having an asthma attack, and she had forgotten to bring her inhaler. We rushed to her room, uncertain what to do. We were in a rural setting at high altitude, hours away from a hospital or medical care.

Arriving, I sensed the woman's panic, heard her gasping desperately for breath, trying to fill her lungs. I saw the terror in her eyes. My mind had no previous experience, and was of no help at all, so I dropped into a place where I could receive my body's instructions.

With her permission, I held her head against my chest. I breathed slowly and deeply, hoping she might entrain her breathing with mine. As I stroked her head, I began to rock, my body rocking hers in time with my breath. To help comfort her, I then began humming a wordless tune, like a lullaby.

I had come to love and admire this woman, and to care deeply about her leadership. She was doing environmental justice work, and her asthma was likely a product of environmental injustice. Every particle of my being willed her to live, and I poured my love and desire for her wellness into her, hoping she would relax, yearning for her to recover and be able to breathe. I don't have any illusion that I healed her. But thankfully, after what seemed an endless time, her breathing steadied and slowed.

As she calmed, I laid her head back down on the pillows. I sat beside her, stroking her head and face. When she'd closed her eyes, and was breathing normally, I sank down to the floor beside her bed. Tears were streaming down my cheeks. Wondering about the source of my sadness, I knew this was about more than relief. I knew that the shell of my separateness had cracked open.

I sensed that the barrier that my privilege had created between my head and heart had been pierced. I felt the pain of this woman's asthma and the profound injustice of her having to live with it acutely. I knew that it was caused due to racial bias, redlining and corporate greed and malfeasance, and my heart ached even as my anger was kindled to change it. In that instant, I also knew my own complicity and accountability for it.

No matter how many years I'd known about the most toxic industries being sited in poor inner-city neighborhoods, and the suffering that results from the toxic inequities, corruption and corporate abuses of our current systems, no matter how long I'd known about the elevated rates of asthma and diabetes, of heart disease and cancer in these communities, I had known them from the distance my privilege afforded me. I had known them as statistics that shocked and saddened me, but I had never before felt the direct impacts of that injustice the way I did so personally that night.

After holding her in my arms, rocking her and breathing with her, summoning every bit of love and will I could muster, I'd felt no difference between us. The mother bear within me had been wholeheartedly engaged, and my desire to stand with her fully, to see her live and thrive had broken my heart wide open.

This experience changed me, as others have continued to do since. They not only widened the scope of what I feel in service to, they deepened my compassion and commitment toward justice. Justice has become personal for me. The author/educator/activist Cornel West suggests, "Justice is what love looks like in public."

These experiences remind me to invest in my heart's experience when hearing another's suffering, and to focus on *feeling* injustice, not just *thinking* about it. And they remind me to encourage others to practice deepening their own capacity for empathy. For cultivating both a thin and a thick skin, at once. For cultivating the muscle to witness and feel the suffering of others and ourselves, while staying present, separate and well-resourced in our capacity to respond to it. Rather than feeling overwhelmed, incapacitated or guilty when confronted with others' suffering, I believe we must develop ways to be both compassionate for it, knowing its seeds live inside of us as well, and aware of our own choices in responding to what we know will only change with our honest and resourced engagement.

PATHWAYS FOR REPAIR AFTER RUPTURES

Best Practices (Notes from the Journey)

O n the deepest level, my core impulse has always been about healing relationships with our selves, each other and with Mother Earth. I see them as all being octaves or fractals of the same societal imbalance or cultural inheritance. Since this is a time of so much polarization, conflict and social turbulence, many pathways for repair are calling for attention and learning. My life and experiences have drawn me to respond to a particularly intractable problem: the tendency of well-intended diverse groups to rupture, even as they attempt to organize toward a common goal. As in the instance below, this then fractures and decimates their capacity for coalition-building, or for coordinated and aligned action.

In my work co-creating connection among diverse women leaders, I've experienced many such ruptures that have happened around differences of race, class and privilege. Many times, my own blind spots have been revealed to me. This series of humbling "ahas" has kept me continually aware of how much I have to keep learning, and of how much of others' lived realities I need to continue to explore to increase my empathy, understanding and effectiveness.

A close colleague and work partner of mine in recent years has been Rachel Bagby, an award-winning vocal artist/composer who graduated from Stanford Law School with a concentration in Social Change. Rachel has mentored girls and women leaders to unleash their voices as instruments of transformation for over 30 years. Originator of the poetic form Dekaaz, she is the bestselling author of *Daughterhood*, and *Divine Daughters: Liberating the Power and Passion of Women's Voices*.

Together, we've delivered trainings designed to strengthen the voices and collaborative skills of the national dairy cooperative Organic Valley's women leaders and shared leadership of three other gatherings, intended to seed enduring relationships among diverse women leaders. The spectrum of differences we address in our work together is not only diverse in ethnicity, but also across age, class, nationality, sexual orientation and issue area. The first two trainings were quite successful, and affirmed the need to initiate long-term relationships resulting in good alliances and mutual aid.

The third gathering, in 2015 — almost from the very beginning — ruptured and splintered repeatedly around issues of cultural appropriation, in ways that were intractable, seemed unresolvable, and felt immensely painful. Cultural appropriation (or misappropriation), I continue to learn, refers to the experience that happens when people of a dominant culture emulate, borrow or integrate practices that were sourced from minority cultures in ways that are sometimes deemed disrespectful and hurtful to people, particularly Indigenous cultures and their allies, especially due to a history of colonial rule.

While it's an issue with much complexity and many perspectives — as some Indigenous people I know feel that the best thing that

could happen on Earth would be for all non-Indigenous people to
adopt Indigenous worldviews and perspectives — I've also come to
understand cultural appropriation as being excruciatingly painful for
some people of Indigenous descent.

The group that gathered in 2015 included non-Indigenous
people whose work in the world had been mentored, inspired and
trained to include Indigenous practices, as well as others who were
Indigenous by birth and practitioners themselves. In my naïveté, I
had imagined that, because the former had been knowingly mentored
and given permission by their Indigenous teachers, these women's
work would not be seen as offensive to others. In fact, the differences
between them, and the unresolved wounding that was opened as a
result, felt intractable. The title of this training was "Comadres," a name
that I'd been careful to cite as being inspired by and borrowed from
Latina culture, and which referred to a sacred and lifelong relationship
occurring between women. As it turned out, the name also ignited hurt
and anger as an example of my having appropriated something sacred
from another culture.

For four days, anger, blame and judgment continued to rupture
and divide the group circle. Although there was significant facilitation
skill among the group, and we tried repeatedly to reset, regroup and
reorient the field, it proved to be impossible.

Although many who had attended said they were grateful
to have been there because of all that they'd learned, and everyone
stayed through to the end, I was devastated afterward. I searched
my soul in the months that followed, and identified places where
my own privilege and naïveté had blinded me and caused me to
invite participants who I otherwise might have known might trigger
each other. I took responsibility for my part, extending apologies

and making amends to all that I could, in varying and, I hope, meaningful ways.

As I discussed it at length with Rachel, we realized that this was not an isolated incident but represented a pattern that had plagued progressive movement-building for decades. I recalled the early emergence of the environmental justice movement, when low-income, Indigenous and communities of color began organizing around the systemic pattern of the most toxic industries being sited where they lived, perpetuating terrible health impacts. I recalled how large public foundations had brought leaders of many groups together, hoping to strengthen their organizing through coalition-building, only to have the gatherings rupture repeatedly. I've come to understand now that those ruptures were likely due to two dysfunctional systems clashing: the foundations and the nonprofit sector. The foundations may not have had the expertise, savvy or skillfulness to convene such a gathering successfully, perhaps expecting outcomes prior to knitting together real alliances and relationships. The nonprofit leaders were likely exhausted, appropriately frustrated by the challenges they faced, and damaged through the daily pain of their work. Sadly, they were also likely competing with each other for scarce resources. Our social culture thus far has habituated us more for competition, unfortunately, than for cooperation.

As my mentor Dawna Markova taught me, all relationships go through rupture and repair. I learned from her that the resilience and durability of any relationship is determined by the nature and quality of its rupture and repair, and so I began to turn my attention to that process.

In order to encourage learning in relation to rupture and repair, we decided to bring together a group of seasoned professional facilitators — women who had deep experience in coalescing diverse groups to find common cause — in a peer community. We began to consider it as a Community of Practice, a group that might collaboratively help reveal and cross-pollinate insights that could help advance the learning of the field. We sought to explore the potential power of experienced people sharing their own current learnings and challenges in walking the talk of their values and work. We hoped that this group might help to reveal "best practices" among us to help advance or accelerate our learning.

The practitioners we brought together were caringly selected not only for their experience and knowledge base, but also for their level of emotional maturity, self-awareness and vision. They came from Canada, Alaska, New York, New Jersey, Colorado and California. As has become central to our work with Bioneers' Everywoman's Leadership, we sought to optimize diversity in every way. The women ranged in age from mid-thirties to seventies and were ethnically diverse (four of the eleven were women of color of mixed background, including Indigenous lineages, Hispanic, and one from East Asia). Each brought experience working with people in diverse sectors and settings, spanning corporate clients, grassroots and frontline, political (bipartisan), environmental and health-affected communities.

In addition to Rachel Bagby and myself, our group included the following esteemed participants:

- **Anita Sanchez**, PhD, international best-selling author, trainer and speaker;
- **Libby Roderick**, singer/songwriter, Turtle Island Records; director, Difficult Dialogues Initiative, University of Alaska, Anchorage;

- **Ana Sophia Demetrakopoulos**, facilitator, community-based research and social innovation;
- **Teresa Younger**, lifelong activist, policymaker and executive director, Ms. Foundation;
- **Pele Rouge**, Earth Wisdom teacher & guide, co-founder, Timeless Earth Wisdom, Inc.;
- **Sharon Shay Sloan**, culture worker and social healer, executive steward, The Ojai Foundation;
- **Joan Blades**, activist, social organizer, and co-founder, Move On, Moms Rising, Living Room Conversations;
- **Taij Kumarie Moteelall**, artist, activist, social entrepreneur, founder, Standing in Our Power;
- **Jody Snyder**, co-founder and visionary, Earth Matters, Pachamama Alliance facilitator, and convener of diverse groups seeking connection to the land and to each other.

The gathering was designed around practices we've developed through Bioneers' Cultivating Women's Leadership retreats, which encourage leading from the heart: tending to relationships before task. We spiraled in to learn about each other slowly, employing rituals, as we've learned that ritual creates relationship. Unlike most organizational settings, where the planning and strategic work takes precedence, we spent the first days together sharing stories about our lives and works, getting to know each other, eating and laughing, making art and playing games together.

Acknowledging that these participants were both skillful and wise, Rachel Bagby and I framed the gathering by inviting everyone to generate changes or initiate shifts in the program when needed, and to share responsibility for the program, if something needed to change. A sense of strong mutual respect permeated our time together, coupled with curiosity about each other as we co-created a Community of Practice.

We had open-space sessions, where anyone among the group could host whatever they desired to share. Some shared specific practices, while others convened discussion circles to explore next steps in their work. Because the context we co-created was simultaneously flexible while offering the structure needed to encourage intimacy and relaxation, much spontaneous emergence occurred. All felt welcome to bring their dreams, intuition, playfulness and creativity to bear in our work together.

This sense of spaciousness was intentional, as we've learned that the feminine principle in us all thrives in spaciousness. In literal terms, this meant that at the front end of our six days together, we had unstructured time for conversations, walks in nature, experiential work, ritual and play to emerge fluidly and organically. So, when the time came for our "agenda" to elicit best practices, they flowed easily, gracefully and swiftly from each participant out into the room.

One participant taught us an embodied somatic practice of shedding the physical effects of trauma through shaking. It was powerful and cathartic. Afterward, we asked everyone to reflect upon their experience with groups, to consider what had worked in setting up the conditions to repair hurt feelings and damaged relationships after a rupture had occurred. I suggested that each of us write lists in our journals, and then we shared them verbally with the group. The question I invited each to write about, to discover what each practitioner knew, was "What do we know about creating conditions conducive to connecting meaningfully across differences that often divide us?"

Some practices came in the form of agreements that were suggested to solicit or share with a group at the beginning of a convening. Still others addressed the form and prerequisites for the meeting, and the ways of relating that were most conducive to repair, after ruptures occur. The wisdom and common sense gained from this wealth of experience still awes me and fills me with gratitude.

I'm pleased to have been given permission to share this abundance of ideas, and for those who wish to read it, the full list of practices is included in a subsequent section, at the end of this essay. Of course, each person facilitating a group has his or her own unique style and purposes, so not all of the many practices offered below will resonate equally, but my hope is that much here may prove useful. Asking whatever people you may be working with for their best ideas is always wise, as I've found that groups often learn best what they are able to discover for themselves, rather than what they're taught by a facilitator.

As I've reviewed the abundance of reflections offered, a few themes have emerged clearly for me as Pathways for Inoculating to Avoid Rupture Among Groups that are Diverse in Experience, Power or Ethnicity, or Repairing When Ruptures Occur:

Transparency in naming and valuing differences. This pertains to many aspects of this work, in that appreciating the complexity, value and kinds of diversity in the room gives everyone permission to show up in his, her, or their full uniqueness. This might include class, faith, ability, education and sexual orientation as well as power and privilege, immigrant status, ethnicity, age and political persuasion. Naming some of the differences (and if possible, creating time and space for participants to share stories about their backgrounds) gives all those present permission to bring their own uniqueness fully into the conversation.

Name power dynamics and privilege differentials clearly and up front. Naming how privilege confers blinders, and reminding people that we all have inner victims and perpetrators as well as privilege helps to keep people from polarizing. If possible, having a facilitator share a vulnerable example of his or her own learning helps make space for others to follow.

Clear agreement on the intention, purposes and desired outcomes for the meeting. This correlates to the first theme, as it means making explicit the common goals that are shared by the diverse group and the purpose for gathering. It's important that all can agree to a goal of reaching some higher purpose together, perhaps common ground, or sense of kinship. This also relates to the importance of selecting carefully who will be invited to participate in a group.

Establish and agree to group norms and codes of ethics. This describes "how" we'll be together; which might include being brave, offering feedback generously and kindly, honesty, practicing self-awareness, deep listening, pausing for reflection before responding, and what to do when ruptures or "ouches" occur.

Encourage embodied awareness, as our bodies rarely lie. Often, I've found, a heightened awareness of body sensations can help keep people in the room during an uncomfortable conversation. Physicality is a great equalizer, and it helps keep people grounded in their sensations and emotions, and out of conceptual, reactive or habitual frameworks.

Suggesting deep breaths, and filling our bodies with dignity prior to unpacking an "ouch" can really help people to stay present in the room.

Representation matters — in facilitation or leadership, as well as in the composition of the room. Many people need to feel flanked by others who look somewhat like them to feel supported and to be fully authentic and present.

Prioritize relationship before tasks. Taking the time to establish whole-person relating among participants, in a deep way rather than only through superficial connections, can make all the difference when all is said and done. Although we're all products of a culture that has tended to devalue relationship, or relegate it to the realm of the "feminine," I believe it's now essential to cultivate community, collaboration and coalitions. This has proven invaluable in many groups and situations, and I strongly advocate for the value of overcoming the impatience and cultural bias that tends to assign relationship-building too low a status in establishing priorities for group work.

In addition to gleaning some best practices, we knit a community of practice together, and learned a lot about how to do that. Reviewing all that was accomplished, I am aware that we actually achieved more than we'd ever intended. Coming from a culture that tends to separate and divide us, I believe that gathering communities of practice to knit practitioners together is a potent and powerful act that offers great promise for advancing all our work. In these complex times, we are all asked to be more embodied in translating our values into behaviors, and not just expressing them as ideologies or positions on paper. Everything we can do to get better at this offers high value to the challenges we collectively face.

The cross-pollination of ideas and experience can accelerate learning for others working to help coalesce groups across differences, while addressing the isolation that many in leadership often feel. It connects a network of colleagues who can call upon each other for coaching, listening or support, as needed. Each can receive the gift of experiencing group learning through reflection and sharing which is in itself a shift in ways of doing things, a healthy evolution of revolutionary work. Being able to refocus our internal and collective capacities on learning from and with each other and away from the incessant call of the "problems" was in itself a gift that opened new horizons. And a community of practice can offer care for those who so often are giving far more than they're receiving, and offer a safe space to rest, renew and process challenging events or emotions.

As I reflect on the trajectory of my learning, and the powerful pull toward purposeful action I feel on behalf of social and racial healing and beloved community, I am struck by one more big realization. Few white people, or people of privilege that I have heard speak on this, have mentioned how profoundly fulfilling and joyous it can be to fully engage in this work.

It's true that it's hard, and often uncomfortable. I'll paraphrase Van Jones who said that if you embark on racial justice work, you just have to orient yourself that it's like walking through a room full of garden rakes. There's no way to cross that room without stepping on one or more rakes, and having their handles spring up and smack you in the face. In my experience, that's a terrific metaphor. I've been amazed at how much instinctual fear seems to arise in me whenever I stretch my own learning edges about race and privilege.

NATURE, CULTURE AND THE SACRED   189

But what's also true — which I've heard far less frequently — is how worthwhile the emotional bumps and bruises of engaging with racial justice have been for me, as a white woman. I've never regretted them. I know I've got lots more coming, as I am sure to continue making mistakes in the months and years ahead.

I've been amazed at the terror I've felt when speaking publicly about cracking the shell of my own privilege, and at including an essay about it in a book. But I am grateful that I pushed through my fear and did it anyway. I am determined to keep taking risks and learning on behalf of the beloved community that is the world I want. There is no other work I see as more timely, needed and vital.

I hope many others get inspired to become intentional rake-walkers and add standing on behalf of racial justice to their committed intents and purposes, in a real, focused and determined way.

For those who might be facilitating groups, I include the entire list of strategies for initiating groups, or attending to ruptures before they happen, that emerged from our circle, below. While some of it will be redundant, I trust that some may find value in them. The practices follow as brief points, with explanation where it seems to add value.

Joan Blades, activist, social organizer, and co-founder, Move On, Moms Rising, Living Room Conversations:
- Culture or expectation of respect, listening, care, dignity and honesty.
- Always meet in person, and with food.
- Make agreements about how to engage.
- Identify shared values up front.
- Practice relationship before task.
- Pause for reflections after connecting.

Jody Snyder, co-founder and visionary, Earth Matters,
Pachamama Alliance facilitator, and convener of diverse groups
seeking connection to the land and to each other:

- Open with discussion about privilege as a culture of
  blinders.
- Model self-discovery about blinders, so people
  understand.
- Bodies as a source of truth: If or when body responses
  arise, attend to them, and encourage others to do so and
  to express what they notice.

Taij Kumarie Moteelall, artist, activist, social
entrepreneur, founder, Standing in Our Power:

- Use discomfort as an opportunity for self-inquiry.
- Meet people where they are.
- Articulate the challenge and suggest choosing to be
  both thick-skinned and thin-skinned at once. This
  means practicing not taking things personally, or getting
  defensive, while also being empathically sensitive, to be
  able to feel what others may feel.
- Celebrate diversity as a path toward oneness.
- Establish how much both individuals and the community
  care about outcomes.

Pele Rouge, Earth Wisdom teacher and guide, co-founder,
Timeless Earth Wisdom, Inc.:

- Design the time with spaciousness, for amplifying
  learning, relaxing, discovery.
- Create inner and outer beauty.

- Invite inquiry and curiosity.
- Remember that relationships require their own time, they cannot be forced or rushed.
- Ensure that all voices are heard and respected.
- Encourage all to come from a place of deep respect.
- Create agreements that protect and encourage safety and trust.
- Create protocols about "oops" and "ouch."
- Agree to keep the energy clear and bright.
- Approach disagreements with transparency.
- See differences as a signal to expand the boundary.
- Note a need for strong inner structures as outer structures are crumbling.

Teresa Younger, lifelong activist, policymaker and executive director, Ms. Foundation:

- Promote common understanding that time is different for everyone; some take a while to settle in.
- Offer opportunity to pass if one doesn't wish to speak.
- Consistency in language re: understanding and different terminology.
- The person who holds responsibility for continuing conversation may not be the one who made a triggering statement.
- Exercise caution re: assumptions about gender norms, and articulate conscious inclusivity.
- Be accountable to those agreements; how will they be held?

Anita Sanchez, Ph.D., international best-selling author, trainer, speaker:

- In lieu of safety, encourage instead conditions for brave conversations.
- Create structured experience re: deep listening.
- Refer to "Dignity" as spoken by Bishop Desmond Tutu.
- Facilitators need to name and model diversity.
- Training about inner awareness and relationships, with modeling.
- What do you want?
- Balance program design and flexibility.
- Holding space of difference and commonality with full mutual responsibility.
- Acknowledge sacred space.

Libby Roderick, singer/songwriter, Turtle Island Records, director, Difficult Dialogues Initiative, University of Alaska, Anchorage:

- Ask about gender pronouns.
- Use storytelling.
- Deploy caucusing as needed.
- Feedback that is ongoing and continuous (anonymously if needed).
- Pre-agreements.
- Never have someone be the "only...."
- Structures that allow people to reveal multiple identities.
- Set up practice duos/pairs.
- Recognize that we all carry oppressor and internalized oppression within us.
- Ask everyone: What do you want? Not want? Be explicit.

Sharon Shay Sloan, culture worker and social healer,
executive steward, The Ojai Foundation:

- Healing can only happen in the present time, so
  encourage addressing "ouches" in real time, in the
  spirit of mutual support.
- Reconciliation is always on the agenda and is essential.
- Establish multiplicity and pluralism as truth of our realities.

Ana Sophia Demetrakopoulos, facilitator, community-
based research and social innovation:

- Agreements = Code of Conduct.
- Accountability, all sign on for agreements.
- Set a goal of mutual visibility.
- Establish a group norm of ability to speak with deep
  honesty, without discounting the other person or
  harming the relationship.
- Encourage clarity, re: I-statements, you and we
  (valuing subjective experience).
- Creation of shared experiences that validate and
  strengthen shared values.
- Creating conditions for people to experience healthy,
  loving and mutually supportive social and relational
  connections.
- Creating good conditions for safe expression of
  vulnerability.
- Create context to be able to address the personal, the
  interpersonal and the structural.

Nina Simons and **Rachel Bagby**, co-facilitators of Women
Cultivating Leadership retreats:

- Step Up — This is a common precautionary suggestion
  used to remind people to check their habitual patterns. It
  suggests, because privilege is often invisible to those who
  benefit from it, that if you are someone who commonly
  speaks first, and often, to notice it, and so to hold back.
  And if you are someone who commonly waits to speak
  up, to exercise the muscle of stepping up.
- Name and appreciate differences, especially those that
  describe power and privilege differentials, up front
  and clearly, as it can ease tensions felt by those who
  perceive them (typically those with the least power
  and privilege).
- Make agreements with the group about what's needed if
  unintended hurts or mistakes happen, framed as "ouches"
  and "oops," and agree about the need to address them
  quickly, if and when they do occur.
- Suggest participants practice exquisite and ongoing self-
  awareness about the blinders that tend to accompany
  privilege in any form.
- Propose practicing sensitivity and care in inviting
  collaborative education, and frame the experience as a
  "learning field."
- Data shows that a minimum of thirty percent of any
  minority needs to be present in order for its members to
  feel flanked enough to fully show up.
- Reflect the diversity you seek to encourage in leadership
  of the group.

- Be kind and authentic, not "nice."
- Encourage a feedback-rich environment.
- Monitor (self and others) re: conditioned responses, like white guilt or shame, victimhood, blame or fix-it mode.
- Encourage all to feel embodied and present, with dignity.
- Encourage inquiry and risk-taking from all present.
- Before speaking, to check yourself, and your intentions first, to see "What will further the relationship?" This helps to avoid comments that blame and shame.

The lists above are lengthy, as I preferred to offer you all of it, unedited. As such, they contain far too many points to be readily adopted and integrated into anyone's practice in their entirety. In reviewing them, however, I realize that these abundant offerings will continue to inform my self-awareness, as well as my work in convening groups in the years ahead. I trust that as you read and review them, those that are most useful to your situation, place and time may also help to guide your efforts. I am deeply thankful to the women who so generously contributed them.

My hope and prayer is that these practices may help to repair or ameliorate the ruptures that will come — inevitably, as we've been so thoroughly socialized and traumatized to perpetuate them — so that the work of cultivating connective tissue among our diverse constituencies to co-create a just, healthy and regenerative world for all can help us to operate as a beloved community. There are few things I believe are more urgently needed now and in the future.

WOMEN FINDING VOICE

The Relationship between Inner and Outer Work

(A Conversation with Terry Tempest Williams)

Terry Tempest Williams may seem at first glance to be a paradoxical figure — part desert mystic and defender of wildlands and creatures who is comfortable alone deep in the wilderness; part scientist and scholar with a highly refined literary and artistic sensibility; and a woman strongly tied to her family's deep roots and Mormon religious heritage in Utah, and yet also a modern dissident and sophisticated, cosmopolitan citizen of the world. As such, she perfectly illustrates that amazing weaving of factors that makes for a transformative leader, in my view.

I am honored to also call Terry a beloved sister, friend and teacher, and she's helped me understand a new relationship to paradox: she's taught me to eschew either/or solutions, to find ways to dance with and celebrate apparent contradiction, rather than being seduced by some effort to resolve it. In embracing all those parts of herself, she's blazed a pathway for each of us to celebrate our own inherent diversity.

She's most often thought of as one of America's greatest nature writers, and though her work defies comparison, she belongs in the illustrious company of John Muir, Aldo Leopold, Rachel Carson, Gary Snyder, Barry Lopez, Annie Dillard, and Henry David Thoreau. She has won many of the most prestigious literary awards, but her writing explores and illuminates so much of the human condition that it transcends any categorization.

Her writing poetically and soulfully traverses the domains of love, family, activism, religion, art, nature and the quest for healing and meaning. Witnessing how many passions and ways of being Terry weaves together into coherent narratives has given me greater permission to navigate multiple domains and systems at a time. Because of course, it's all one system.

She has long been recognized as one of our greatest defenders of wildlands and passionate advocates for peace, environmental and social justice, and freedom of speech. Her activism has taken many forms, from acts of civil disobedience on a nuclear test site to marching in the streets to testifying about women's health before Congress, to doing something only she could pull off: quoting Mormon scriptures to explain the wild desert's spiritual essence to a room full of stunned Republicans.

What is most inspiring to me about Terry is her essence, her being, her awakened presence, the penetrating authenticity and inquiry she brings to every encounter and conversation. This is a woman who is emotional, vulnerable, passionate and ferociously engaged, but she is so deeply centered, so attuned, so refined, so devoid of any reactivity or malice, and radiates such intense dignity and purity of soul that her words have the potential to reach deeply into even hardened human hearts. From *Refuge* to *Leap*, and from *Finding Beauty in a Broken World* to *When Women Were Birds*, her books never fail to illuminate the invisible web that connects the world anew for me.

This podcast, hosted by Bioneers Everywoman's Leadership program, was a conversation between Terry and me that took place in July 2012. In it we explored how women find voice, as well as the relationship between inner, reflective work and outer, activist work. Our conversation braids together so many threads and themes that have arisen throughout this book previously, pointing to essential aspects of leading from the feminine, including the practice of relationship intelligence, deep listening and the power of emotions and grieving. I hope you'll find yourself resonant with it, and may even find some new wrinkles or clues that help illuminate your path forward.

Nina Simons: Terry, I am thrilled to be able to talk with you about some of the ideas in your beautiful book When Women Were Birds, *and to visit with you as someone who has been a really profound influence and role model and mentor for me in my life in finding my own voice.*

Terry Tempest Williams: Nina, I can say the same back to you. You continue to mentor me about what women's leadership from the heart looks like, sounds like, feels like. I will just honor you.

NS: Thanks for that. Hard to receive from someone I love and respect as I do you, but I hope it is getting easier as I practice. For me, what I have realized is that finding my voice has been directly connected to finding my own sense of purpose, or assignment, or that unique set of instructions that feel like they are mine to do. I was so moved by a quote in your book, Terry, where you wrote that your mother Diane said: "There are two important days in a women's life. The day she is born and the day she finds out why."

As I've witnessed the arc of your last fifteen years or so, it struck me that perhaps, like me, your sense of assignment keeps unfolding. It is not like it lands fully blown in your lap and you suddenly know what you are born to do. For me, it is more like crossing a river, where I step on a stepping stone and I know that is the right place for me to step but I can't see the next step until I am fully there. My instructions keep emerging over time. I wonder whether you will be willing to share any reflections you might have on your instructions and unique purpose.

TTW: That is so interesting that you shared those words, instruction and purpose. And honestly Nina, I don't think about that. What I am aware of is what I love, what I have lost, and what I have tried to reclaim. For me it is very simple: it's a question of really being present in the moment. If we are present in the moment, then we know what to do.

NS: Well, then let me offer you a reflection on one of the things that I feel I have learned from you and keep learning from you: how to bring all the parts of myself into full presence in the moment. When I reflect back over your last several books, it seems that in each book you share something about what guided you into that exploration of presence.

In Finding Beauty in a Broken World *you talk about how you asked the ocean for some words. What I notice about you, Terry, is that you seem to be very good at listening for guidance from somewhere either deep inside yourself or in the natural world or both. I wonder if you have any idea how you learned to listen so well.*

TTW: I remember after September 11th, you and I talked about this. I was in Washington, D.C. when the twin towers were struck, when

the Pentagon was hit. I witnessed people running across the White
House lawn and I was with a group of photographers at the Copland
Gallery and we found ourselves stunned as I know everyone was.
The next thing I knew, we were in a cab in gridlock and the cab
driver turned around and asked, "Where would you like to go?" I
realized there was no place to go. We were there.

That next year I made a conscious commitment to speak the
truth as I saw it. I realized there are many forms of terrorism and
environmental degradation. But during that year I realized my voice,
my critique, had become as brittle and as hollow as those as I was
opposing.

It was at that point that I went to the ocean. I addressed
the ocean spirit, however we define that, and I said, "Give me
one wild word, and I promise I will follow." So perhaps you are
correct in using that word instruction, because the word that came
back to me, the word that I heard in my own heart was "mosaic."
It became a seven-year journey, following what mosaic is, how do
we take those pieces that are broken and make something new,
something whole.

With this book, *When Women Were Birds*, you know what
I was listening to? I was listening to the very real fact of my
uncertainty about my own mortality, realizing that I had turned 54,
the same age my mother was when she died. I really was looking
back and remembering what I had chosen to deny, that my mother
left me all her journals before she died and all her journals were
blank. And so, the book becomes a reflection and meditation, a deep
listening, to what that emptiness might have meant.

NS: What inspires me in you is the way that you listen both for the ocean,

for the spirit of the natural world, as well as for what's most alive and
questioning and wondering and burning in yourself.

TTW: I think it is about survival, don't you? I mean, both of us are
in very privileged positions but life is not easy. If we are interested
in an evolution, a revolution of the spirit, then I think it demands
that we ask these hard questions and that we stay with them. That we
don't avert our gaze, that we sit with the uncertainty. Revelations do
come, but not without a cost, not without patience, and not without
compassion for ourselves and for those that we live closest with.

NS: I agree, and I find for myself that the older I become and the more
aware I am of my own mortality, the more burning the questions become.
As I age, the more my desire to fully manifest the artwork of my life or the
assignment that my soul was given in its fullness burns in me. Because we
live in a time of so much transformation, and so much loss and so much
suffering, I feel called to bring my "all" in response to that. I also feel an
increasing need to not shrink away from what most frightens me. I think
you've modeled that for me.

TTW: You know, I think of my grandfather when he said, every day
counts. I was just in Madison, Wisconsin on the eve of the Scott
Walker election recall. There was such angst on both sides about
what would happen. Mat Rothschild, the editor of *The Progressive*, is
a friend of mine. We ended up that morning at dawn going out to
Picnic Point Nature Preserve and we watched birds. I cannot tell you
the glory of the moment when, as we were talking politics, wondering
what was going to happen, suddenly we heard this incredible
prehistoric call. We both smiled and a sand hill crane flew right over

us, we could have touched his or her legs. You know, you think, "Nine million years of perfection just graced us," and it really does put things into perspective.

NS: Yeah, it sure does. I am curious to lean toward the reconciliation of paradox because just as you were saying, Terry, part what prompted you to write When Women Were Birds *was the legacy of your mother's journals and how her voice was reflected in the emptiness of words on those pages. I find myself so drawn to the inquiry of how we unlock from paradoxical duality.*

For me, one of the most important capacities we can look to develop is how we connect across difference. And you have modeled that for me, Terry, in so many ways, from adopting a grown man from Rwanda as your son, to studying prairie dogs up close and personal for weeks. You model it by helping us understand their world by going inside it and writing about what you learned. I am curious about any thoughts you may have about how we connect across difference and the value of it in this time.

TTW: Nina, I am struck by the words "reconcile" and "paradox," and I am not sure that I ever reconcile anything. I think I embrace paradox. I grew up on the edge of the Great Salt Lake, a body of water in the American West that nobody can drink because it is salt water. So, I think I am very comfortable with paradox.

I grew up in the Mormon church, which is very patriarchal, and yet all the women around me were unbelievably powerful. You know, paradox. It is true, Brooke and I are childless by choice and suddenly, at 50 years old, I find myself adopting Willy into our family and re-defining what family looks like. You know, I am not Willy's mother and he is not my son and yet he has allowed me to be a mother. To understand what it's like to have your complete heart, soul, mind embodied by another person out of regard, and love, and care and often times, confusion.

I gravitate towards what I have loved. I think I am most interested in what is other than myself. I know who I am, and I am much more interested in who you are and what this world around us feels like, looks like, tastes like; what it is like to touch. I think it is my curiosity that keeps moving me forward.

NS: Of course. As another woman who is childless by choice, you have helped me understand that whether or not we have biological children, we all, and I suspect regardless of our gender, we all can have the essence of parenting and mothering and loving another person so much that they become a part of our being.

TTW: I think that is right. I was having a conversation this morning with a dear friend of Brooke's over coffee. How do we expand? How do we amp up our frequency? I can speak this language with you.

I am very well aware of the desert. When we first moved to Castle Valley from Salt Lake City, Utah, five hours south, it took me several years to feel that my body was in frequency with the desert because the vibration in the desert is so high.

You know this from living in Santa Fe, Nina; very little is hidden. You are living in this very erosional landscape and it is asking of you to be bare-bone and exposed. I keep thinking with all the changes that are happening on the planet right now, with all that we are asked to take in, how do we keep expanding and allow ourselves greater porosity, so that we don't shut down, so that we don't become numb, so that we can continue to engage. That is the question that I am living with. At times, it feels like it is too much and yet as you say, I want to be of use. I want to be alive, awake, and alert to that which surrounds me.

NS: For me, that requires that I keep giving myself the permission to feel as deeply as I do, because I am mindful that we live in a culture where that permission is somewhat rare. And as a woman, I have often felt derided or ridiculed for being emotional. What I am learning is that actually that love is the source of my strength, and my wisdom, and my power. And that in order to celebrate life — which I really think is part of why all human beings are here on the planet at this time — we have to allow ourselves to feel the loss and the pain of witnessing as what we love is diminished and threatened.

TTW: I so agree. Such power in what you are saying. What kind of human being we would be if we were not feeling this grief, if we weren't being emotional about the lives and the life before us.

I was thinking about abuse and I believe that we really are in an abusive relationship with the feminine, however we define it — whether it is emotion, truth-telling, anger or understanding, or maybe silence — the feminine in all its diversity. I often find that we are minimized, trivialized, invalidated, we are discounted — that makes for craziness. So often, what I feel inside is not mirrored on the outside, and that makes me crazy.

And when we are talking about voice, we really do have to stand in the center of authenticity and realize, "No, this is what I am feeling. And, no, I will not allow you to minimize my thoughts or my actions. And, no, I will not allow you to discount me."

We cannot do it alone and yet we try to do it alone. That is why I think community is very important and this is why I so appreciate what you have put together with your program. We cannot do it alone. I so appreciate what you have done with Everywoman's Leadership and Cultivating Women's Leadership because it shows that there is a community of women and this is what leadership from the heart looks like. It gives all of us the courage to follow our instincts and our intuition.

NS: I find myself feeling increasingly supported in the awareness that what the feminine offers us is the capacity to flex with changing conditions. To live with uncertainty. If there is a key to cultivating our whole humanity and our voice and our leadership, it has something to do with how we stay connected, and how we live with uncertainty. So, I wonder if you have any thoughts about that because you have lived with so much, Terry.

TTW: Nina, I think a lot about Wangari Maathai, who passed on too soon, on September 26, 2011. I think about the uncertainty that she lived. As an African woman, as a woman in Kenya, in a very patriarchal society, what was certain for her was that women were carrying the environmental crisis on their backs and that an environmental crisis is an economic crisis, is ultimately a crisis of social justice. That was certain to her. She saw it, she felt it, she witnessed it.

What was certain for her was that women could change the course of their lives and what was certain for her was the faith of a single seed. I love that and now, you know, how many millions of trees have been planted because of her love and her capacity to grieve for what we were doing to the planet?

Again, it is that paradox. What is certain, what do we know and what is uncertain and what we will never know? You know, none of us knows how long we are going to live. That is the first great uncertainty but we know that we're alive, that is a certain thing. You and I are speaking to each other. So again, it is a dance, this balance, this scale. And I love how even the brush of a feather can tip that balance. So, I want to live with that feather.

NS: It is so beautiful because it is the power of the small and the particular to make big change...

TTW: Truly.

NS: What you are saying gets us back to the dance of paradox. I am reminded that nature's way of resolving paradox is a spiral. That when you pour cold milk into hot tea, the difference in their temperatures gets resolved by a spiral, whether you stir it or not. Just the liquid does that. When the seaweeds are dancing in the ocean current, they spiral in order to be resilient. It is a dance, not a marriage, or a reconciliation.

TTW: I love that. You know, there is spiral all around us. Perhaps that is the nature of paradox. I went out with Willy and his friends to the spiral jetty out on the shores of the Great Salt Lake and it struck me how profound that form and that metaphor is to progress, to evolution, to revolution.

NS: I also find myself wanting to appreciate what Wangari did, which was that she kept speaking even though she knew it meant incurring wrath and anger and violence to herself...

TTW: Even being separated from her children and hoping that they would understand and forgive her for what she was taking on. Again, that word "courage." As she often would say, it was not courage, it was just what needed to be done. Recently, I was talking with a student of mine about the definition of courage. She said, and I love this: to her, courage is sustained focus. For her courage is that. Don't you love that?

NS: It's beautiful. Because what we appreciate appreciates. I recently attended a memorial service for a dear friend and a remarkable activist who died too young and I found myself so aware that like you, she brought celebration to the fight for justice. Always. I noticed as I was speaking at her memorial, how rare that is, because the fight can so often engender bitterness and anger and we can shut down because it is so hard. And the beauty and the power of staying connected to what you love, even as you are putting your body, your voice and your heart into helping to ignite change, is something I admire so much.

TTW: Yes. I just was at Dartmouth for the last three months. One of the most special days was being on the Dartmouth Green during the Powwow. Dartmouth was one of the first colleges in the country to honor Native people and Native American students. This was the 40th Powwow they have held on the Green. For two days I sat next to the singers and I just felt their drum beat going up my spine. In all the celebration of shell dancers, the jingle dancers, it was so thrilling, and yet, again the paradox, you don't know but you imagine the difficulties of the lives on the reservations. Having worked in Navajo Country, I know this is America's hidden wound that we have never fully acknowledged, and yet, when I think about the deepest humor I have experienced, it's been from my Indian friends. And, when I think about the really dark humor with my own family, it's come out when we were facing the death of a loved one. Again, it's about survival, and we all have these evolutionary skills. I think rituals — singing, celebration, dancing — all these things help us move in that spiral of what it means to be human. Often, we seem to be caught in a downward spiral, an entropy of work and scale. Lately, all I hear is: we need to work to scale or scale up, and I just keep thinking really, can we just scale down? I just do not understand that. I just find myself wanting to get quieter and quieter and smaller and smaller.

NS: [Laughter] Well, and your book invited me into a meditation in such a beautiful way because I want to be slower and stiller, and you know, it is the blur of fastness and pressure and too muchness and busy-ness, that causes me to miss the particularity and the beauty and sacredness and the humor that you are talking about.

TTW: And then we end up being tired, and angry and resentful and we have all been there. More and more, I just want to be still. I also think about Robert Pinsky when he says "motion can be a place too." But my mother always talked about being the nest behind the waterfall. How do we find that core of stillness in our heart so that we can, again using your words, fully appreciate where we are here and now.

I think it is tied to voice and to paradox. When I was writing *When Women Were Birds*, I thought I was writing a book about voice, about how we as women speak to the truth of our times, to our own authentic nature. But what I have written, Nina, is a book of silences and stillness and I think one begets the other. Again it is that balance of space and time and scale.

NS: Well, I find myself aware that the need for silence is also a marker of the imbalance between the feminine and masculine in our culture and in all of us. I was just speaking to a friend the other night about the unfinished wounding in the conquest of this land. The huge destruction that has been wrought on Native peoples all over the world and also the wounds of slavery, of sexism, racism and ageism. How do we encourage and invite the healing that can come from naming and ritually pouring our love into addressing all those wounds? I see them as fractals of the same tear in our relational fabric.

TTW: Again, love is not the secret. Pain is. And why are we so fearful of that? Because I really believe if we embrace our pain we can move beyond that. Again, I am scratching my head. Here we have a president that we have supported and admired, Barack Obama, and I will certainly be voting for him again. But with a community of people we have been trying to embrace the Arctic to preserve this reservoir for our spirit, and yet it is Barack Obama and his administration that has opened up the Arctic for oil and gas drilling. They have opened the door to Shell.

Just last week in *The New York Times*, they were talking about how Shell has been very sensitive to the Native American people when in truth, I have an Alaska Native student who has been working with her father to stop drilling in the Arctic, to stop drilling in the Arctic Ocean. They are buying off Native Americans with trucks with boats and anything else you can imagine. So, what do we do? I keep thinking, do we lay our bodies down? Is it the time for direct action and yet how do we still proceed with calm and understanding? I don't know what the answers are. And that is the paradox where I find myself torn, by my anger and by my love, and sometimes I think they are the same thing. So, what do we fight for, and what do we accept?

NS: Yes and how do we recognize that not only our pain deters us but our shame and complicity as well.

TTW: The only way I can reconcile the paradoxes of action and contemplation — and I'll use that word "reconcile" now — is in discernment. To me the power of discernment is most potently rendered in our own communities, on our home ground with our own people. That is where it is the toughest to speak truthfully because we cannot walk away from our friends and family.

NS: What you're naming so beautifully is the complementary wholeness that is created by combining contemplation with action, and that unless they are met in full measure, it is not the full humanness that I aspire to.

Terry, you've said that you "do not believe we can look for leadership beyond ourselves." Can you talk a little about what that means to you in both your personal and professional work and how you maintain the connection between the two?

TTW: It is such a good question. I am going to refer it back to you Nina.

NS: [Laughing] It is such a hard question and such a good question. What's clear to me is that the landscape that I can be the most responsible for is the one that lives within me. I need to keep challenging myself, I have to keep finding the spaces that scare me and the places that I have anger and actually lean into them so that I can find ways to bring myself into congruence.

I keep crafting myself inwardly as if there is a social sculpture in my own life that is me, and I am the only one that can make this artwork come out the way I hope and intend it. When I began to understand the extent of harm as a result of the invisibility of racial injustice to many people of privilege in this country, I began to realize that even though it terrified me to talk about it, I actually had to push myself towards that edge and find ways to challenge myself to step into it.

For me, weaving the boundary of personal and professional, the inner and the outer and the activist, feels like to me like it is the work of my life. And I observe you traversing that ground with quite a bit of grace. So, what do you think?

TTW: I have been very aware that my view of leadership is not the same as the traditional view of leadership: the kind with one powerful person at the top, who we follow. That is not the kind of leadership I am interested in. I'm interested in: What does leadership of the heart look like? What does leadership rising out of the community look like?

I think the Occupy movement has showed us an organic form of leadership where each voice has its own strengths and radiance. That takes time. We're used to top-down decisions, we're used to saying a leader is decisive and doesn't care what other people think. I am interested in a circle of leadership, in spiral leadership, in organic leadership that emerges out of community.

I'm also wondering, Nina, about how we can lead ourselves forward in courageous ways that sustain us and the people that we love. It takes self-reflection and accountability. If we want our country to change, we have to be asking how we change ourselves. The quote that you read from goes on to say that if I want my country to change, how do I change myself.

I was interested in a review of *When Women Were Birds* that appeared in *Christian Review* that the reviewer, male, said, "This woman must have written this book while looking in the mirror and mistook indulgence for literature." I mean, that is pretty harsh. It's interesting that if a man is self-reflecting, culturally we view that as wisdom, but if a woman is self-reflecting then we view it as self-indulgence. So, I think that goes back to those traditional models of what we imagine leadership and wisdom to look like, the all-knowing or the all-questioning. And I would rather exist in the questions.

NS: Terry, I wonder how you navigate the challenge of balancing your service to the world with adequate self-care? I am so motivated by my love and I think because we as women have so much cultural conditioning that tells us to equate our value with what we can give, or how well we serve others, it is easy to give more than we can replenish.

I just find myself actually relying on the wisdom and love and reflection of friends and sisters who encourage me to take time off, who remind me of the value of stillness and self-care. I keep telling myself that we are in a marathon here, this is not a sprint. If I want to bring myself with this much passion, presence, and commitment, I have to take care of the instrument, myself. I need to find ways to ritualize and practice and strengthen my capacity to care for myself at the same time. What about you Terry?

TTW: I agree with you, Nina. We've all been there. I'm thinking a lot about source. What is the source of our joy, what is the source of our pain, what is the source of our strength? And each of us answers that differently, I'm sure. For me, my source is my solitude, my marriage, my community of sisters and friends. My ultimate source is in nature — birds, plants, lying on the ground as barefoot and as exposed as I can be on the hot sand in the desert or walking in the forest barefoot, with that soft, yielding soil underfoot. Just water, ocean, shell. So again, it's discernment, it's assessment, it's all the things we have been talking about, each in our own way and in our own time, with the gifts that are ours.

NATURE, CULTURE & SPIRIT

Integration and Congruence
through Practical Magic

S ince the poems, essays and interviews you have read span ten years of my life, I offer this closing piece to share a current synthesis of my learning from listening for leadership.

Many among us are reaching to cultivate our best selves in the most regenerative and effective ways to help heal our ecological and social systems, and shift the course of our ailing world, while also celebrating and enjoying life. My hope is that this offering might prove useful to cultivating your own emergent or evolving leadership.

While some of the chronic biases and injustices of our social systems are increasingly visible to many — across economics, race, environment, gender, class, age, orientation, ability and ethnicity — the harms and violence resulting from them are also escalating. And, as we are also the immune system of the planet, people are mobilizing, thankfully, and acting on behalf of what we care most deeply about. Now is definitely the time.

That movement-building, however, is still more factionalized than it needs to be, which keeps us from becoming optimally effective. To cultivate our best opportunities to shift our systems, bridge-builders and connectors are needed across all sectors and issue areas to help create connective tissue among diverse yet related communities and constituencies.

And of course, the impacts of our escalating imbalances are not evenly distributed. The harms and violence being felt by some are far worse — due to color, class, nationality, gender, or faith — than for those of us with the privileges that whiteness, wealth or maleness still confer. In the global south, refugees fleeing their homelands due to climate change impacts and violence are increasing, even as white nationalism is spreading. Thankfully, many individuals and communities are stretching and boldly risking much to help alter our course, with approaches as diverse as running for political office, engaging people through the arts, as well as grassroots and movement organizing.

Many more of us now are seeking clarity for how best to develop ourselves to protect and defend what we love. We're heeding a call to act on behalf of a future where diversity in all its forms is valued for the strength and resilience it can offer, and life's creatures and living systems can thrive along with our kids and grandchildren.

What's at stake? Only the capacity of Earth to sustain human life into the future. Many more of us now know that our personal and global health, human rights, peace and freedom — and a viable future and quality of life for humankind — are not only interdependent but are also hanging in the balance.

With all the current challenges of our broken social systems, over the coming years the impacts of climate destabilization will rapidly and inexorably increase the challenges that lie ahead. Potable water and healthy food may become increasingly hard to access, and costly, as droughts and wildfires, tornadoes and earthquakes roil any perceived sense of safety we may have left.

There are no guarantees and we cannot know the outcomes, but I am heartened by my faith that together, with all of our resilience, love and inner knowing, we can "bend the arc of the moral universe toward justice" while we grow our community connections and alternative support systems to help sustain us through the times ahead. One thing's for sure — we cannot do this work alone. We need the power of collective and community for the work ahead.

I am immensely grateful for the emergence of gender fluidity and the dissolving of old gender norms and identities that are increasingly prevalent among younger people. Life has also taught me to appreciate the unique value of caucus work. When people who identify as sharing a gender convene with others who mirror many of their lived experiences, potent healing and strengthening can happen. This has proven valuable in race and class work, as well as with gender.

I realize that — coming from a different generation — my focus on women and balancing gendered qualities in our institutions and culture may seem outdated to some. If so, I apologize for my blind spots, and ask you to receive these ideas flexibly and with understanding.

For the remainder of my days, I will act toward co-creating the world I want, in collaboration with others who share many of my values. For me, this means working to advance the leadership of women, and all people leading more from their "feminine" aspects and an integrated wholeness of our humanity. It also means shifting our culture to achieve greater gender equity and balance in our institutions, cultures and policies. This is the most comprehensive and systemic way I can see to help us to heal on every level — ranging from the individual to the societal and from the social to the ecological.

I am not alone in this perception. Public awareness, in many parts of the globe, is changing far sooner than governance, policies and institutions. Increasingly, researchers, think tanks and survey data are also proving that the leadership of women — and those who lead in a more gender-balanced way — is our best shot toward shifting our course toward a future that's Earth-honoring, equitable and vital.

For example, research by the United Nations has concluded that where women are more educated and participate more in leadership, every aspect of community life improves, from the ecological to the economic.

Sex and World Peace by Valerie Hudson and Bonnie Ballif-Spanvill draws clear correlations between the number of women at the negotiating table in positions of power and achieving regional and world peace.

Paul Hawken's recent book, *Drawdown*, which identifies the one hundred best approaches for lowering carbon in the atmosphere, cites the rights, well-being and education of women and girls as the sixth and seventh most powerful strategies to reduce and slow the impacts of climate change globally.

Nature is all about relationship. It operates through often invisible mutualities and symbioses, ways that different species interact that have reciprocally beneficial outcomes. Win-win solutions create sustainability. It's also a system that's informed by abundance. Like a mother who won't refuse nourishment to her child, when in balance, nature provides us and all of life's creatures with abundant water, air and food to eat.

How might we learn from her model? What if we prioritized relationships over tasks? What if we recognized that the only economy that's trustworthy is the one that's about deepening our relational currency, our social capital, the web of relationships we can rely upon for mutual aid? In reimagining economies, and reviewing what's worked over millennia in some Indigenous communities, the Gift Economy model has emerged, which has many resources and scholarship available online.

Here I offer just a few suggestions for practices and priorities that might prove useful, as you cultivate your own leadership to best serve what you most love:

- Start or join a women's circle, or a men's group. When in aligned, honest and caring relationship, women (and men) have a remarkable (and often under-recognized) capacity to strengthen and heal each other. I began a circle after witnessing a friend's accelerated learning as a result of her own eight-year experience with a circle, and I could feel how profoundly it had influenced and helped her grow. It's not hard. I selected five other women I liked and wished to know better, and invited them to meet, so that we could co-create what kind of a circle might best serve our desires and needs. Once together, we jointly created priorities and purposes and agreements, and we were on our way.

- Practice listening actively, not only with your ears, but with your whole body and attention. Listen with focus and full presence to others' stories, and listen at least as much as you talk.

- Create room in your activities for brief periods of rest and spaciousness — throughout your day. Just a few minutes can replenish and regenerate you.

- Get to know your neighbors, or invest some time and energy in showing up for and with your local community. The more you are intimate with a circle of friends or community, the more that circle is likely to strengthen you, and to show up for you or your family when you need them.

- Learn about your own ancestry, so that you can develop a connection to your own lineage, as we're all indigenous to planet Earth. Then, listen inwardly for dreams or other flashes of inspiration that might be coming from your own ancestors.

- Pay special attention to the surprising impulses, dreams or flashes of inspiration that visit you. We all receive information differently, and the more you come to know, and attune to, your own ways of listening, the better your chances of hearing and responding to the guidance you receive.

CULTIVATING CONGRUENCE THROUGH PRACTICAL MAGIC

To heal the imbalances in the world, I believe we must first unearth and address those mirrored within ourselves. It's helped me to acknowledge, vulnerably and with humility, where the same patterns of ranking, polarization and judgment that I see out in the world live within myself.

As long as I can remember, a benchmark for my own personal learning and growth has been congruence. A life aim of mine is to bring the many disparate parts or aspects of myself into alignment; like braiding many strands into a coherent whole. I seek to be present with the same authenticity no matter where or with whom I show up. I hope that the council of Ninas that lives inside my psyche can get ever better at hearing each other, and at integrating their diverse voices toward coherence. One of our deepest human needs is to belong, so perhaps my quest for integration and congruence stems from a desire to have all parts of myself be accepted, present and accessible.

So much of what has previously defined womanhood has centered around our adaptability and responses to other people's needs, desires and realities. My desire for liberation from that pattern prompts me to want to reach a sense of belonging fully to myself, and also to all that I love.

At the same time, in a complementary way, my sense of safety lies in belonging in relational community, being held by a web of relationships with people who I know fully hear, trust and appreciate me, even with my blind spots and shortcomings.

This goal of inner integration asks me to identify, reconcile and nourish healthy versions of the feminine and masculine within me. An example: my "masculine" conditioning taught me to work hard and long to accomplish much in short periods of time, without adequately attending to my body's needs for the rest, sensuality, creativity and spaciousness that my feminine character requires. Seeking equilibrium has required me to take a long, hard look at the ways my insecurity causes me to perpetuate my overachieving behavioral habits in a quest for external validation. As I learn to value myself and my work more, I can better tend to my disparate needs.

I'm learning to replace that need for external validation with inner appreciation; practicing relational mindfulness, and creating disruptive opportunities to enjoy periods of play, creativity, self-care and friendship time. Relational mindfulness is a version of meditation (and a book) that its creator, my colleague and mentor Deborah Eden Tull, calls "the subtlest form of self-love." It was her adaptation, after seven years as a Zen monk, to find integration with herself, and to cultivate practices for regenerative leadership. Practicing it helps me to stay centered under stressful circumstances, and connected with all my senses, emotions and ways of knowing.

About ten years ago, I received a teaching from a Peruvian shaman named Oscar Miro-Quesada. He led a very long ceremony, lasting seven or eight hours, during a solstice. At the very end he said:

> *"If you remember only one thing from this time, remember this:*
> *Consciousness creates matter*
> *Language creates reality*
> *Ritual creates relationship."*

This teaching lodged in my heart and mind, and the more I considered it, the more useful I found it to be. I consider it as offering guidance for practicing practical magic.

Here are some examples of how it's become helpful to me, in my quest for integration and congruence.

CONSCIOUSNESS CREATES MATTER

Recently, as I've been recovering from a hip replacement surgery, I experienced some ways that the invisible world influences the material

one. Before the surgery, my caregiver and friend Linda suggested we do
a ceremony to express gratitude and say goodbye to my old hip joint. It
felt so good to do that, as it's an important part of me that's served me
well for over sixty years.

Knowing that scientific studies have affirmed the effects of
nonlocal healing — of people praying for those undergoing hardship or
injury — I asked many friends to send me love and prayer and envision
me wrapped in light during my surgery. As I fell into an anesthetized
trance, I felt their prayers holding me, palpably.

As my body repaired, I spent time each day visualizing the
tissue, skin and bones of my hip healing, and also poured love with
intention and focus into my new hip. I encouraged my body to accept
these new bionic parts, inwardly. My healing process progressed faster
than anyone had predicted or believed possible.

When I spend a few minutes in the morning, before leaving bed,
imagining how I hope my day will greet me, I am often well met by
events and delighted by synchronicities. I'm also practicing visualizing
and sending prayers, as my lived experience keeps validating that it has
influence. The sacred I believe in and pray to is all around and within
me, and throughout nature.

LANGUAGE CREATES REALITY

As I become more conscious of my choices of phrases and words, I can
cultivate my congruence. The language we've inherited is filled with
violence and gender bias. For example, instead of describing efficiency
as "killing two birds with one stone," which perpetuates a kind of
numbness toward violence, I've learned from my colleague Rachel
Bagby to instead say "feeding two birds with one scone."

In women's groups, I notice how often we refer to each other as "guys," and it troubles me. I prefer to say "women" or "gaias" instead. People often refer to humanity as mankind, and as a feminist, I prefer to use the word humankind, as it includes everyone. We have a lot of creative renaming to do, to reshape our world.

After learning about climate change through Bioneers over the past twenty-nine years, when I hear people frame it as a crisis about "saving the planet" I wince, knowing that their language is not accurate or true. Earth will survive, no matter what we do, though it may take millions or billions of years for it to recover. The climate crisis we face is about saving humankind. It's actually about how we do or don't create conditions for humanity (and many other species who are being lost due to our resistance to make change on the scale that's needed) to be able to exist or thrive on Earth.

For me, each of these language choices have become real and important, and I try to practice listening for where my language may be out of alignment with my heart's vision for co-creating the loving, equitable and truthful world I yearn for.

RITUAL CREATES RELATIONSHIP

When I realized that I was perpetuating harm to myself each morning, by inwardly critiquing my body as I looked at myself in my bathroom mirror, I decided to experiment with the use of ritual to alter my pattern, and perhaps even create some new neural pathways. My purpose: to cultivate a kinder relationship to my body.

I invented (and continue to practice) a ritual to cease judging myself on a daily basis, and instead pour love into my physical being. I mix up body oil with moisturizer and essential oils whose scents

please me, and when I step from the bath or shower, in lieu of self-
judgment I anoint my body with the oils, as I thank every part of it
for the ways it serves and supports me. I hold myself accountable for
doing this every day.

One ritual we've used in women's intensives works whether
practiced for yourself or to help connect a group. We call it "Compost
and Cauldron," and it's a way of naming and claiming what you are
cultivating to strengthen in yourself and may be also sharing for the
benefit of the group (that's the cauldron part, for what we're cooking,
together) and what you may be consciously shedding, letting go of, or
composting, to return it to the Earth to serve as nourishment for life.
Each in the circle speaks when and if they're inclined, and speaking
to the center says "I'm composting my ___(eg: desire to please others
ahead of tending to my own needs, fear of facing conflict, or whatever
may be true for them), and I'm putting in the cauldron the courage I
felt yesterday when...." The quality of truth being shared can be tender
and deep, as people recognize the shared reality of challenges or issues
we often face. It deepens relationship among a group, as well as within
oneself.

I've noticed — after creating and practicing several kinds
of rituals to alter patterns I've observed in myself — that I reach a
time about four weeks in where I question whether it's making any
difference. When I accept that uncertainty, but remain firm in my
commitment to keep practicing, I typically notice that somewhere
between six and eight weeks, I can feel a difference in my behavior, and
in my psyche.

Each of these practices is strengthening my belief in and
capacity to engage with the invisible world. And, while the examples
I've shared are personal and individual in nature, I believe the same

principles apply to larger visions and intentions related to our
ecological and social systems.

I am learning — in spite of society's conditioning to the
contrary — to remember, respect and listen for the guidance of the
invisible world, the energetic realms, what I perceive as practical
magic. Through practice and attention (and guided by my intention
to get better at this) I'm improving my ability to listen, from all sorts
of sources. Sometimes images or messages arrive in dreamtime, or just
as I awaken, as an idea that pops in fully formed. I'm not always sure
whether it's coming from ancestors or guardians or intuition, but I'm
learning to listen for it and respect it, regardless of its source.

I learned recently of a renowned scientist whose study of
consciousness led him to believe more strongly in the power of the non-
physical world. David Bohm, a physicist and colleague of Einstein's who
studied with spiritual masters including Krishnamurti, suggested that
reality is actually comprised of two realms of activity, which he called
the explicit and the implicit order.

The explicit, he said, is everything that we can perceive with our
five senses, everything in the "material" world.

The implicit, on the other hand, is everything else, what's
invisible and inaudible through our physical senses and therefore seems
unprovable through the scientific method.

Most people, he noted, presume that the explicit — what's
physically palpable to us — is the larger field by far, and has the greater
influence on events in the world. However, his research revealed a very
different perspective on reality.

The metaphor he used to describe the actual relationship
was this: Imagine that the explicit order — all that we can perceive
physically — is the foam that arises on the waves of the ocean. It comes

and goes with the waves, winds and tides. The implicit order, he said, is the entirety of the sea itself. What's not perceivable to our senses actually regulates — in his metaphor — not only the waves, the tides and the foam, but the whole of Earth's weather system itself.

For me, Bohm's observation helps me counteract the negative voices in my head, the habituated biases that say "take time for setting intention, meditation and visualization? There's far too much to be DONE." Coming as it does from a smart white man, it helps to affirm my intuition and body's knowing that attending to the invisible world is vitally important to affecting social and ecological healing, and flips my inherited bias on its head.

INTEGRATION AND RECONCILING APPARENT CONTRADICTIONS

Our U.S. culture has had a propensity for separating people, ideas or elements into categories and stressing their differences, often positioning them as opposing or binaries. One example is: activism and citizen engagement of all kinds, which often gets juxtaposed with and deemed superior to inner, reflective work like meditation or energy approaches that emphasize setting intention, visualization, prayer or receptivity.

This false separation we've been habituated to, that ranks the value of activism as being superior to more inwardly-focused work, runs contrary to what I believe is needed for navigating this transformative time. If the conjoining of the two — engaging both the material, explicit world and the invisible, implicit one — might be so much more powerful than either one practiced separately, isn't that worth considering?

In lieu of the "divide and conquer" strategy that's been the norm for so long, we need to practice finding commonality across differing backgrounds, perspectives and faiths. What if we focused on learning how to value our differences, rather than exploiting and aggravating them?

To influence a transition from a culture founded upon a win-lose hierarchical paradigm to one based upon collaboration, mutual respect, equity and love, we've got to reveal the false dichotomies that are embedded throughout our thinking and our language. The essence of our work involves shifting from a society based upon conflict, concentrating power, ranking and violence, to one based upon complementarity, shared authority, appreciating diversity and peaceful collaboration.

Many Indigenous cultures suggest that the time we are in — a time between worlds or octaves of realities — asks humanity to shift from a form of leadership that's led by analysis, intellect and our minds, to a leadership that's guided by the heart's wisdom.

We are culturally shaped and therefore implicitly biased, so that we navigate the world by ranking the guidance of head over heart, since centuries of Western culture has reinforced that perception. In recent years, however, science is revealing how much our hearts actually determine our physiological, psychological and neural responses, determining our capacity to respond to life and to self-regulate.

Of course, neither of these examples — action and spirituality, or head and heart, can exist in their best form without the engagement and dance of the other. Sacred activism and wisdom-informed, heart-led action is what's actually called for. As Terry Tempest Williams and I reflected in the piece before this, these apparent paradoxes are actually meant to be embraced. Our challenge is to learn to have them dance together, to complement each other. Like the sun and moon, nature's design is based upon complementarity and reciprocity, and is not composed of binaries or opposites.

Just as nature resolves conflict or contradiction through spirals, so must we. In nature, as Janine Benyus (the founder of the emergent field of biomimicry) informs us, the places where different ecosystems meet are the spaces of greatest fertility and innovation. Where the river meets the ocean, and the grasslands meet the forest — it's at the conjoining of two worlds that new invention is most fruitful.

In a time when the very future of the human experiment on Earth is in jeopardy, doesn't it make sense for us to bring all the best of our human capacities into alignment, and into congruence, to ensure the greatest outcome? Why not learn to dance with the apparent paradoxes that appear to us, or to "call BS," as the youth from Parkland High School modeled so courageously, when we're presented with false separations that diminish our authority and undermine our collective power as change-makers?

As children of Mother Earth and the moon, and women whose cycles naturally align with the lunar phases, I believe we are all designed by nature to attune to her guidance, if only we will listen and heed her counsel. The future of humankind on Earth, and of many of our non-human kin, may depend upon it. Thankfully, it's also the most fulfilling, congruent and joyful way to dance with life along the way.

I hope you'll join me in exploring this nexus, this dance of apparent contradictions. Together, may we co-create the community and connective tissue needed to help us travel the arduous path ahead. After all, as Clarissa Pinkola Estes notes: *We were born for this.*

ACKNOWLEDGMENTS

M y deepest heartfelt thanks to Kenny Ausubel, my beloved partner and co-creator, who often sees possibilities for me before I see them myself, as he did in suggesting this book. I will always be grateful to my editor, writing partner and friend, Anneke Campbell, whose soul purposes are so aligned with my own, and whose skill and discipline help make this work flourish.

My heartfelt thanks to Sharon Zetter, whose skill and aesthetic discernment as a book designer are such a gift to this, and to all the books she designs and co-creates. I bow in gratitude always to my beloved friend, activist and artist Mayumi Oda, whose glorious image graces this cover and so embodies the leadership I'm listening for. Thanks to the team at Bioneers, and all whose caring contributions and editing input have directly helped to make this book better, more whole and beautiful.

I am grateful always to my ancestors and family: to my magical mother, Rhea Goodman, whose joyful and creative life models "Living Juicy" like no one else. To my loving brother, Tony Simons, who continues to help shift business culture towards greater integrity, with devotion and perseverance. To my nephew, Cole, whose kind and sensitive leadership will take us into the next chapter. And to my father, Barnett Simons, whose love and artistry gifted me with such a solid and resilient foundation.

I offer thanks to my many beloved mentors and friends whose innovative paths have opened possibilities for my own. Many of those named below are mutual mentors and friends in my life, so these categories are somewhat arbitrary. Some have influenced me in person, and others through your artworks, including especially: Terry Tempest Williams, Alice Walker, Jeannette Armstrong and Marlowe Sam, Toby Herzlich, Rachel Bagby, Elsa Menendez, Sarah Crowell, Akaya Windwood, Claire Wings and Wola, Deborah Eden Tull, Marion Weber, Taij Kumarie Moteellal, Jodie Evans, Joanna Macy, Eve Ensler, Deena Metzger, Starhawk, Susan Griffin, Ohki Simine Forest, Dawna Markova, Diane Haug, Ana Sophia Demetrikopolus and Joy Harjo.

A web of friends who hold me with constancy and enduring love, who buoy me when I get low: Zuleikha, Lana Holmes, Pele Rouge, Lorraine Weiss, Kate and Jeff Haas, Jody Snyder and Noel Littlejohns, Sarah Cavanaugh, Maggie Kaplan, Joan Porter, DeeAnn Downing, Mary Jonaitis, Polly Howells, Satya Kirsch, Ginny McGinn, Kristin Rothballer, Laura Loescher, Amanda Coslor, and Melissa Engestrand.

Lastly, I wish to thank all the women who have participated in my wild and sometimes bumpy evolutionary ride: to the UnReasonable Women for the Earth, to all the magnificent alumna of Cultivating Women's Leadership, to those who have trusted Rachel Bagby and myself in gatherings named Comadres, Wisdom Council and Community of Practice, and the people who have engaged in our workshops on Leading Through Relational Mindfulness: Regenerating Ourselves and Our World, with Deborah Eden Tull. Thank you for the gifts of your time, your trust and your presence. May all of our leadership help shift our course, and transform our culture.

Photo by Genevieve Russell

NINA SIMONS, the co-founder of Bioneers, is a social entrepreneur passionate about reinventing leadership, restoring the feminine, and co-creating a healthy world for all. Nina is co-editor of *Moonrise: The Power of Women Leading from the Heart*, and a contributor to *Ecological and Social Healing: Multicultural Women's Voices*. She co-facilitates transformative leadership intensives and retreats on regenerative leadership through relational mindfulness. Nina received a Robert Rodale award in 2003 and was a recipient in 2017 of the Goi Peace Award. For more information on Nina's work, and to learn where she may be speaking or teaching, please visit ninasimons.com.

ANNEKE CAMPBELL has worked as a midwife, nurse, yoga teacher, English professor, poet and scriptwriter. She recently co-authored (with Thomas Linzey) *We The People: Stories from the Community Rights Movement in the U.S.* and co-edited (with Nina Simons) *Moonrise: The Power of Women Leading from the Heart*. She co-produced, with her husband Jeremy Kagan, the dramatic feature film *Shot*, which she also scripted.

SELECTED BIBLIOGRAPHY

*For access to the full resources (people, organizations, and media)
referenced in* Nature, Culture & the Sacred, *please visit:
www.ninasimons.com/resources*

Alexander, Michelle. *The New Jim Crow: Mass Incarceration in the Age of
    Colorblindness.* The New Press, 2012.
Amini, Fari, et al. *A General Theory of Love.* Vintage, 2001.
Ausubel, Kenny. *When Healing Becomes a Crime: The Amazing Story
    of the Hoxsey Cancer Clinics and the Return of Alternative Therapies.*
    Healing Arts Press, 2000.
Bagby, Rachel. *Divine Daughters: Liberating the Power and Passion of
    Women's Voices.* Harper San Francisco, 1999.
—. *Daughterhood: Sounding Hidden Truths, Ignite Your Freedom.*
    Amazon Digital Services LLC, 2016.
Benyus, Janine. *Biomimicry: Innovation Inspired by Nature.* Harper
    Perennial, 2002.
Bohm, David. *Wholeness and the Implicate Order (Volume 135).*
    Routledge, 2002.
Campbell, Anneke and Nina Simons, editors. *Moonrise: The Power of
    Women Leading from the Heart.* Inner Traditions International, 2010.
Capra, Fritjof and Pier Luigi Luisi. *The Web of Life: A New Scientific
    Understanding of Living Systems.* Anchor, 1997.
—. *The Systems View of Life: A Unifying Vision.* Cambridge University
    Press, 2016.
Caprioli, Mary, et al. *Sex and World Peace.* Columbia University Press, 2014.
Coates, Ta-Nehisi. *Between the World and Me.* Spiegel & Grau, 2015.
D'Antonio, Michael and John Gerzema. *The Athena Doctrine: How
    Women (and the Men Who Think Like Them) Will Rule the Future.*
    Jossey Bass, 1994.

Einstein, Albert. *Einstein on Politics: His Private Thoughts and Public Stands on Nationalism, Zionism, War, Peace, and the Bomb.* Edited by David E. Rowe and Robert Schulmann, Princeton University Press, 2013.

Ensler, Eve. *The Good Body.* Villard, 2005.

—. *The Vagina Monologues.* Villard, 2007.

—. *In the Body of the World: A Memoir of Cancer and Connection* Picador, 2014.

Estes, Clarissa Pinkola. *Women Who Run with the Wolves: Myths and Stories of the Wild Woman Archetype.* Ballantine Books, 1996.

Garcia, Alixa and Naima Penniman. *Climbing Poetree.* Whit Press, 2014.

Harris-Perry, Melissa V. *Sister Citizen: Shame, Stereotypes, and Black Women in America.* Yale University Press, 2013.

Hawken, Paul. *Drawdown: The Most Comprehensive Plan Ever Proposed to Reverse Global Warming.* Penguin Books, 2017.

Hill, Julia Butterfly. *The Legacy of Luna: The Story of a Tree, a Woman and the Struggle to Save the Redwoods.* HarperOne, 2001.

Hill, Julia Butterfly & Jessica Hurley. *One Makes the Difference: Inspiring Actions that Change our World.* HarperOne, 2002.

LeGuin, Ursula K. *Dancing at the Edge of the World: Thoughts on Words, Women, Places.* Harper & Row, 1989.

Macy, Joanna. *Coming Back to Life: Practices to Reconnect Our Lives, Our World.* New Society Publishers, 1998.

Markova, Dawna. *Collaborative Intelligence: Thinking with People Who Think Differently.* Spiegel & Grau, 2015.

—. *Reconcilable Differences: Connecting in a Disconnected World.* Spiegel & Grau, 2017.

Maté, Gabor. *In the Realm of Hungry Ghosts: Close Encounters with Addiction.* North Atlantic Books, 2010.

—. *When the Body Says No: Understanding the Stress-Disease Connection.* Wiley, 2011.

Maturana, Humberto. *The Circularity of Life: An Essential Shift for Sustainability*. Jane Cull, 2013 (preface).

Merton, Thomas. *Conjectures of a Guilty Bystander*. Image, 1968.

Pert, Candace B. *Molecules of Emotion: The Science Behind Mind-Body Medicine*. Simon & Schuster, 1999.

Poo, Ai-jen. *The Age of Dignity: Preparing for the Elder Boom in a Changing America*. The New Press, 2016.

Proust, Marcel. *In Search of Lost Time*. Modern Library, 2003.

Reed, Donna. *The Burning Times*. National Film Board of Canada, 1990.

Rifkin, Jeremy. *The Empathic Civilization: The Race to Global Consciousness in a World in Crisis*. Polity Press, 2010.

Strobel, Leny Mendoza. *A Book of Her Own: Words and Images to Honor the Babaylan*. Tiboli Publishing, 2005.

Tull, Deborah Eden. *Relational Mindfulness: A Handbook for Deepening Our Connections with Ourselves, Each Other, and the Planet*. Wisdom Publications, 2018.

Twist, Lynne. *The Soul of Money*. W. W. Norton & Company, 2017.

Whelan, Linda Tarr. *Women Lead the Way: Your Guide to Stepping Up to Leadership and Changing the World*. Berrett-Koehler Publishers, 2011.

Wicks, Judy. *Good Morning, Beautiful Business: The Unexpected Journey of an Activist Entrepreneur and Local-Economy Pioneer*. Chelsea Green Publishing, 2013.

Williams, Terry Tempest. *Refuge: An Unnatural History of Family and Place*. Vintage, 1992.

—. *Leap*. Vintage, 2001.

—. *Finding Beauty in a Broken World*. Vintage, 2009.

—. *When Women Were Birds: Fifty-four Variations on Voice*. Picador, 2013.

Wilson, Edward O. *Biophilia*. Harvard University Press, 1984.

Yeh, Lily. *Awakening Creativity: Dandelion School Blossoms*. New Village Press, 2011.

ABOUT BIONEERS

A s the world hurtles from urgency to emergency, we can move from breakdown to breakthrough. We can shift our course to reimagine how to live on Earth in ways that honor the web of life, each other and future generations.

Bioneers highlights and helps realize the profound transformation already taking hold around the globe: the dawn of a human civilization that partners with the wisdom of nature's design, and practices values of justice, diversity, democracy and peaceful co-existence. Around the world in diverse fields of endeavor, social and scientific innovators have been developing and demonstrating far better technological, economic, social, and political models inspired by the wisdom of the natural world. Human creativity focused on problem-solving is eclipsing the mythology of despair.

Since 1990, Bioneers has acted as a seed head for the game-changing social and scientific vision, knowledge and practices advancing this great transformation. As a community of leadership, Bioneers is helping disrupt our current failed institutions by offering people better choices. We show a compelling vision, practical models and "the how," through our annual national conference, award-winning media, local Bioneers conferences and initiatives, and leadership training programs.

ABOUT GREEN FIRE PRESS

Green Fire Press is an independent publishing company dedicated to supporting authors in producing and distributing high-quality books in fiction or non-fiction, poetry or prose. Find out more at **Greenfirepress.com**.

Other Green Fire Press titles you may also enjoy:

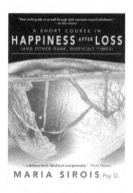

A Short Course In Happiness After Loss, by Maria Sirois, PsyD.

A lyrical gem of a book, combining positive psychology with the wisdom necessary to thrive when facing life's harshest moments, rising through pain into a steady, resilient and open heart.

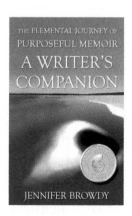

The Elemental Journey of Purposeful Memoir: A Writer's Companion, by Jennifer Browdy, PhD.

Month-by-month guidance for memoir writers.

Winner of the 2017 Nautilus Silver Award.

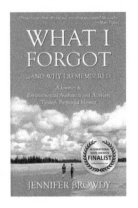

What I Forgot…and Why I Remembered: A Journey to Environmental Awareness and Activism Through Purposeful Memoir, by Jennifer Browdy, PhD.

"Inspires us to see how we can reclaim our lives for the sake of life on Earth" –Joanna Macy.

Finalist for the 2018 International Book Award.

Writing Fire: Celebrating the Power of Women's Words, edited by Jennifer Browdy, Jana Laiz and Sahra Bateson Brubeck.

More than 75 passionate women writers share their voices and visions in this powerful anthology.

Wisdom Lessons: Spirited Guidance from an Ojibwe Great-Grandmother, by Mary Lyons

The culmination of a lifetime steeped in Indigenous spiritual traditions, Grandmother Mary offers invaluable lessons for anyone interested in living in alignment with their higher self.